Abraham Lincoln
The Complete Book of Facts, Quizzes, and Trivia

By
Gordon Leidner

BURD STREET PRESS
SHIPPENSBURG, PENNSYLVANIA

The acid-free paper used in this book meets the guidelines for permanence and durability of the Committee on Production Guidelines for Book Longevity of the Council on Library Resources.

For a complete list of available publications
please write
Burd Street Press
Division of White Mane Publishing Company, Inc.
P.O. Box 708
Shippensburg, PA 17257-0708 USA

Library of Congress Cataloging-in-Publication Data

Leidner, Gordon, 1954-
    Abraham Lincoln : the complete book of facts, quizzes, and trivia / by Gordon Leidner.
        p. cm.
    Includes bibliographical references.
    ISBN-13: 978-1-57249-235-6 ISBN-10: 1-57249-235-X (alk. paper)
    1. Lincoln, Abraham, 1809-1865--Miscellanea. 2. Presidents--United States--Biography--Miscellanea. I. Title.

E457.909 .L45 2001
973.7'092--dc21
[B]
                                                                    00-068910

PRINTED IN THE UNITED STATES OF AMERICA

Dedicated to
My father:
Harold Carl Leidner of Greenville, Illinois
and
My father-in-law:
Buddy Norris of Bryantown, Maryland

Contents

Introduction

It is commonly known that more has been written about Lincoln than any other American, and indeed more than, almost, any other historical figure. Consequently, it would have been easy to assemble a book of Lincoln trivia that included ten thousand facts, rather than the thousand that are included here.

With this book I wanted to provide the reader with a collection of the relatively undisputed Lincoln facts, presented in a way that would make enjoyable browsing. I also hoped to present these facts in a way that could provide the individual that had never read a Lincoln biography (and perhaps never would) with a fairly complete understanding of his life.

I purposely avoided going into details about the Civil War battles, because these are already covered in several excellent trivia books such as *The Complete Book of Confederate Trivia* by J. Stephen Lang. I tried to concentrate primarily on Lincoln and the important issues, places, people, and events of his life. Rather than always giving a single word answer to the question, I frequently added an extra sentence or two in order to provide the reader with a better understanding of the facts and, I hope, spark some interest in further reading.

In assembling this book of Lincoln trivia, I consulted dozens of the most reliable books about Lincoln. I did not include any facts that I thought to be of questionable veracity. Sometimes even the most reliable of sources can be in disagreement on minutia, however, and when this was the case, I carefully compared them and used the facts from the source that was the most likely to have it right. An example is the question of how much land Lincoln received for his military service in the Black Hawk War. Some of the general works claim he received 200 acres. But Harry Pratt's *Personal Finances of Abraham Lincoln* says that he only received 160, and gives the dates acquired and specific counties in which

the acreage was located. In situations like this, a debate between generally reliable sources, I went with the source that
provided the more specific information.

I am indebted to several Lincoln scholars for their review
of my answers. Nevertheless, for the errors that remain I accept
full responsibility. Thanks to Ed Steers for reviewing my
chapters on Booth and the assassination. Dr. Steers, author
of *His Name Is Still Mudd,* and *The Escape and Capture of
John Wilkes Booth,* is one of the Lincoln world's experts on
the assassination, and I appreciate his taking time out from
his busy schedule.

Thanks to Michael Burlingame for reviewing my chapter
on Lincoln's ancestors. Professor Burlingame is the author of
many books, including a future multi-volume biography of
Lincoln that will be published by Johns Hopkins University
Press in 2003.

Thanks to Jennifer Fleischner of State University, New
York at Albany for reviewing my chapter on Mary Todd Lincoln.
Professor Fleischner is currently working on a book about
Mary Todd Lincoln and Elizabeth Keckley.

Thanks to Michael Maione, the National Park Service his-
torian at Ford's Theatre, for several constructive ideas and
criticisms.

I hope this book proves useful and entertaining to the
reader, as well as serves as a worthy collection of trivia of
one of the most fascinating people in American history.

President Abraham Lincoln

⌂ Ancestors

1. What European country were Lincoln's ancestors from?
2. Who was Lincoln's earliest American ancestor?
3. What was Samuel Lincoln's vocation?
4. Who are the six paternal ancestors of Lincoln, beginning with Samuel Lincoln of Hingham, Massachusetts?
5. Is it true that Lincoln's ancestors were Quakers?
6. What famous American frontiersman was a distant relative of Lincoln's great-grandfather John?
7. How and when did Lincoln's grandfather, Abraham, die?
8. Where was Lincoln's grandfather killed?
9. How old was Lincoln's father when his grandfather was killed?
10. Who saved Thomas from the Indian?
11. Who was Lincoln's mother and where were her ancestors from?
12. Was Nancy Hanks Lincoln illegitimate?
13. What trades did Lincoln's father, Thomas, pursue?
14. When were Thomas Lincoln and Nancy Hanks married?
15. What present-day county is Elizabethtown now a part of?
16. What was the name of Thomas and Nancy's first child and when was she born?
17. In 1840 Thomas and Nancy Lincoln moved from their Decatur farm. Where did they move to?
18. When did Lincoln's father, Thomas Lincoln, die?
19. Did Lincoln visit his father when he was dying?
20. In what year did Lincoln's stepmother die?

✍ Ancestors (Answers)

1. England. Norfolk County.

2. Samuel Lincoln of Hingham, Massachusetts. Born in 1619, he emigrated from England in 1637 during the great Puritan migration.

3. He was a weaver's apprentice.

4. Samuel (1619-1690), Mordecai (1657-1727), Mordecai (1686-1736), John (1716-1788), Abraham (1744-1786), and Thomas, Lincoln's father (1778-1851).

5. No direct ancestor of Lincoln's was a Quaker. His great-aunt Sarah was a Quaker.

6. Daniel Boone. John was related to Boone only by marriage. His half brother, Abraham, married Anne Boone, a cousin of Daniel Boone.

7. He was killed by Indians in 1786.

8. On Long Run in Jefferson County, Kentucky.

9. Lincoln's father, Thomas, was seven or eight years old. He was sitting by his dead father's body in a field when approached by an Indian who intended to abduct or kill him too.

10. Thomas's older brother, Mordecai, shot the Indian before he could reach Thomas.

11. Nancy Hanks, born in 1784. Her family moved to Kentucky from what is today West Virginia.

12. Lincoln believed his mother was illegitimate, and the preponderance of oral history indicates she probably was.

13. Carpentry, cabinetmaking, and farming.

14. June 12, 1806. They were married by Jesse Head, a local Methodist preacher, and built a cabin in Elizabethtown, Hardin County, Kentucky.

15. Larue.

16. Sarah, on February 10, 1807.

17. A 120-acre farm on Goosenest Prairie, in the southern part of Coles County, Illinois.

18. January 17, 1851.

19. No. Earlier when he had thought his father was dying he went to see him, but when he finally passed away he was not present.

20. 1869.

♫ Kentucky Childhood

1. When and where was Lincoln born?

2. What was the name of the farm where the Lincolns lived when their son was born?

3. To where did the Lincolns move in 1811 and why did they leave the Sinking Spring Farm?

4. What was the name of Thomas and Nancy's third child and what happened to him?

5. From which parent did Lincoln inherit his physical and mental traits?

6. What accident almost took Lincoln's life when they were living at Knob Creek?

7. When did the Lincolns move to Indiana, and why did they leave the Knob Creek place?

8. Why did the Lincolns have so many problems with land titles in Kentucky?

9. Could Lincoln's mother read and write?

10. What book did Lincoln's mother read to him more than any other?

✍ Kentucky Childhood (Answers)

1. February 12, 1809, in a log cabin near Hodgenville, Kentucky.
2. Sinking Spring Farm. It was named for a spring near the cabin.
3. To a farm on Knob Creek, about 10 miles northeast of Sinking Spring. They left because of difficulty with the land title.
4. Thomas, born in 1811, died in infancy.
5. From his mother, Nancy Hanks Lincoln. She is said to have been tall and thin, and "very intelligent," although uneducated.
6. He nearly drowned in the creek.
7. In 1816, when Lincoln was seven years old. They left primarily because of problems with the title of their farm.
8. Kentucky never had a US Land Survey, and many claims were made with reference to disputed landmarks. Consequently, there were continuous problems with people claiming the same property.
9. She could read but not write and signed her name with an "X."
10. The Bible.

❧ Indiana Childhood

1. Why did Thomas Lincoln move his family to Indiana?
2. How much land did Thomas Lincoln buy in Indiana?
3. Where did the Lincolns move to in Indiana?
4. What is the present-day name of the county the Lincolns moved to?
5. After moving to the Pigeon Creek area, in what kind of shelter did the Lincolns first live?
6. To what sort of shelter did they move to next?
7. What food did the Lincolns live on their first months in Indiana?
8. What game did Lincoln shoot shortly after his eighth birthday that caused him to swear off hunting?
9. What tool did Lincoln first start using at the age of eight that he would one day become famous for?
10. Not long after the Lincolns moved to Indiana, some of Nancy's relatives from Kentucky moved next to them. Who were they?
11. What other relative moved with the Sparrows?
12. What near-fatal accident happened to Lincoln when he was eight years old?
13. On October 5, 1818, when he was nine years old, Lincoln's mother died. What was the cause of her death?
14. What other relatives of Abe's died from the Milk Sick?
15. Who was Thomas Lincoln's second wife?
16. What were the names of Sarah Bush Johnston's children (Lincoln's stepbrother and stepsisters)?
17. What improvements did Thomas make to the Lincoln cabin after his new wife and stepchildren moved in?
18. What did Lincoln call his stepmother when he was young?
19. Could Lincoln's stepmother read?

✍ Indiana Childhood (Answers)

1. Indiana had been surveyed by the US government and had guaranteed land titles.
2. One hundred sixty acres.
3. Pigeon Creek, in Perry County.
4. Spencer.
5. A floorless shelter of logs, enclosed on three sides but open on the fourth.
6. A one-room cabin with a fireplace, but the winter arrived before they were able to properly chink the cracks with mud and grass. Consequently, their first winter in Indiana was very cold.
7. Wild game.
8. A wild turkey. Killing the bird so sickened him that he later said he "never since pulled a trigger on any larger game."
9. An axe. He was big enough that he was able to cut wood for his father.
10. Elizabeth and Thomas Sparrow, Nancy's aunt and uncle. They moved into the Lincolns' old three-sided shelter.
11. Eighteen-year old Dennis Hanks, who was supposedly the second person to hold Lincoln after he was born. It was Dennis, who while holding his baby cousin, had said that Lincoln "would never amount to much."
12. He was kicked in the head while switching his old mare at a gristmill. Knocked unconscious and bleeding, it was thought that he would die until he awoke four hours later.
13. The "Milk Sick." It was contrived from the milk of cows that had eaten the poisonous snakeroot plant.
14. Nancy Lincoln's aunt and uncle, Elizabeth and Thomas Sparrow, died shortly before Nancy. All three were buried on a wooded knoll a quarter mile from the Lincoln cabin. Lincoln's cousin, Dennis Hanks, moved in with the Lincolns.
15. Sarah Bush Johnston, a widow with three small children. Thomas returned to Elizabethtown, Kentucky, and married Sarah Bush Johnston within a year of the death of his first wife.
16. Elizabeth, John D., and Matilda.
17. Installed a wooden floor, a window, a better door, and a loft for the boys to sleep in.
18. Mama.
19. No. But she brought with her what would eventually be known as the Lincoln family Bible from Kentucky.

20. What was Lincoln's relationship with his father like?
21. What trait did Lincoln inherit from his father?
22. How tall was Lincoln at the age of 16?
23. What happened to Lincoln's older sister, Sarah?
24. What were some of the jobs Lincoln did as a teenager?
25. Who owned the ferry Lincoln ran as a teenager?
26. How did Lincoln earn his first dollar in a single day?
27. When he was 17, who hired Lincoln to go to New Orleans and why?
28. What were "The Chronicles of Reuben"?
29. What vocation did Lincoln ask his friend William Wood help him obtain at the age of 20?
30. Why did Thomas Lincoln move from Indiana to Macon County, Illinois, in 1830?
31. Where did the Lincolns first settle in Illinois?
32. Where was Lincoln's first political speech?
33. When did Lincoln make his second trip to New Orleans?
34. When the people of New Salem first saw Lincoln, what was he doing?

20. Lincoln became alienated from his father at a young age. Thomas Lincoln seemed to favor his stepson, John D. Johnston, over his own son. Lincoln, who grew to value education so highly, disapproved of his father's lack of ambition to learn.

21. His love for storytelling and funny stories.

22. Six feet, two inches. He weighed about 160 pounds.

23. When Lincoln was 17, his sister married a neighbor by the name of Aaron Grigsby. A year later she and her baby died in childbirth.

24. Plowing, splitting rails, blacksmith's helper, store clerk, and slaughtering hogs.

25. James Taylor.

26. He rowed two men out to a riverboat in the Ohio River. They each tossed a fifty cent piece into his boat, and he could "hardly believe my eyes."

27. A merchant by the name of James Gentry hired Lincoln and Gentry's son Allen to take a load of goods via flatboat to New Orleans. Lincoln earned eight dollars a month, plus passage back by steamboat.

28. A poem Lincoln wrote, ridiculing two brothers on whom he played a practical joke. The brothers were married in a joint wedding ceremony, and Lincoln attempted, unsuccessfully, to have them go to the wrong bedrooms.

29. Deckhand on a steamboat.

30. John Hanks had moved to the Decatur area and claimed that land was much more fertile. Also, another breakout of the Milk Sickness in Indiana inspired Thomas to leave and take his family.

31. Near Decatur, close to the Sangamon River.

32. In front of Renshaw's Store in Decatur, Illinois, when he was 22 years old. It was on the subject of improving the Sangamon River for transportation purposes.

33. Summer 1831. A merchant by the name of Denton Offut hired Lincoln and Dennis Hanks to take a load of goods to New Orleans. It was while making this trip down the Sangamon River that Lincoln had his first encounter with the people of New Salem.

34. Trying to get Denton Offut's flatboat off the dam at New Salem. It had hung up on the dam and was filling with water.

⊞ Education

1. Where did Lincoln and his older sister Sarah first attend school?
2. What was the name of their first teacher?
3. Who gave Lincoln his first handwriting lesson?
4. What are the words to the oldest known poem Lincoln wrote as a child?
5. Who was the first school teacher Lincoln had in Indiana?
6. Who was Lincoln's second teacher in Indiana?
7. Who was Lincoln's third teacher?
8. What was the basic curriculum of these schools?
9. What book did Lincoln first use for spelling?
10. What were two of the early readers Lincoln learned from?
11. What was one of Lincoln's earliest history books?
12. What was Lincoln's earliest math text book?
13. How was Lincoln first introduced to Shakespeare?
14. What books did Lincoln read the most frequently?
15. What biographies of famous men did Lincoln read?
16. What book, borrowed by Lincoln from neighbor Josiah Crawford, was damaged by rain?

1. While living in Kentucky at the Knob Creek place they attended what was known as an ABC School.

2. Zachariah Riney.

3. His cousin Dennis Hanks, using a buzzard's quill.

4. Abraham Lincoln/his hand and pen/he will be good but/god knows When. Another poem Lincoln wrote right after this one is: Abraham Lincoln is my name/And with my pen I wrote the same/ I wrote in both hast [*sic*] and speed/and left it here for fools to read.

5. Andrew Crawford. He taught a Blab School about a mile from the Lincoln cabin. Lincoln and his sister Sarah attended Crawford's school for one term.

6. James Swaney. He taught in a cabin about four miles from the Lincoln home. It was so far away that the Lincoln children went only sporadically.

7. Azel W. Dorsey. He taught school in the same cabin as Andrew Crawford had, about a mile from the Lincoln home. Lincoln and Sarah attended for about six months.

8. "Reading, writing, and ciphering 'to the rule of three.'" Ciphering to the Rule of Three meant ratios and proportions.

9. T. Dillworth's Spelling Book, entitled *New Guide to the English Tongue*. It began with two-letter words, followed by three-letter words, then four.

10. *The Columbian Class Book* by A. T. Lowe and the *Kentucky Preceptor* by N. Webster.

11. William Grimshaw's *History of the United States*. Grimshaw's book probably reinforced Lincoln's dislike of slavery.

12. N. Pike's *A New System of Arithmetic*. Lincoln would work out math problems by writing on a board with charcoal and then shaving it clean with a drawing knife. He later sewed a few sheets of paper together to assemble a notebook.

13. From the textbook *Lessons in Elocution* by William Scott—which had excerpts from Shakespeare's plays.

14. The *Bible, Pilgrim's Progress, Aesop's Fables, The Arabian Nights*, and *Robinson Crusoe*.

15. *Life of George Washington* and the *Life of Benjamin Franklin*, both by Mason L. Weems, and the autobiography of Benjamin Franklin.

16. Weems' *Life of George Washington*.

17. What did Lincoln do to pay for the book?
18. What math subject did Lincoln decide to study when he was in his late forties?

17. He pulled fodder for two days. Lincoln got to keep the book, and would later state that it was one of the most influential of his childhood.

18. Geometry. He "mastered the six books of Euclid" so that he could train his mind to think more logically in the courtroom.

⚑ New Salem

1. Why did Lincoln decide to take up permanent residence in New Salem after returning from his second trip to New Orleans?

2. When did Lincoln move to New Salem?

3. How old was Lincoln when he moved to New Salem?

4. What was the name of the local roughneck Lincoln wrestled shortly after he arrived in New Salem?

5. What happened in the wrestling match?

6. What were some of the odd jobs Lincoln initially worked at in New Salem?

7. How did Lincoln acquire the nickname "Honest Abe"?

8. What was the name of the steamboat that came up the Sangamon River to New Salem in 1832, and how was Lincoln associated with its arrival?

9. What happened to Denton Offut's store?

10. After the election, what was Lincoln's next business venture?

11. From whom did Lincoln and Berry buy their store?

12. What did Lincoln read while clerking at the store?

13. What was Lincoln's favorite poem?

14. What happened to the Lincoln and Berry store?

15. After the Lincoln and Berry store failed, what was Lincoln's next job?

16. How much did Lincoln earn as postmaster?

17. Where was the post office Lincoln managed?

✍ New Salem (Answers)

1. Denton Offut thought that New Salem would be a good place to have a general store, and he asked Lincoln to help him build the store, stock it, and work as clerk.

2. July 1831.

3. Twenty-two.

4. Jack Armstrong, one of the "Clary's Grove Boys" from a nearby community.

5. Accounts vary. Some say Lincoln won, and some say Armstrong won. All agree, however, that Lincoln won the friendship of Armstrong and respect of the Clary's Grove Boys as a result of the match.

6. Lincoln ran Offut's store, the gristmill, and the sawmill. He provided some legal counsel to neighbors in the court of the local Justice of the Peace, Bowling Green.

7. When running Offut's store, if he determined he had accidentally overcharged a customer a few pennies, he would lock up the store and walk miles, if necessary, to return the money. He also acted as a judge in contests and wrestling matches, and was so fair that everyone "took his judgment as final."

8. The Talisman. Lincoln acted as assistant pilot from Beardstown to Portland's Landing.

9. According to Lincoln, it "petered out" in the spring of 1832, primarily as a result of poor business decisions by Offutt.

10. He went into partnership with William Berry to establish a general store in New Salem. There were two other stores in the village at the time, but one of the others soon went out of business.

11. Row Herndon. Lincoln and Berry borrowed over a thousand dollars to buy the store and stock for it.

12. Poetry, especially Burns, Holmes, and Shakespeare.

13. "Mortality" by William Knox. It started with the words, "Oh, why should the spirit of mortal be proud?"

14. According to Lincoln, it "winked out." With the population of New Salem diminishing, sales slowed and the store failed in 1833.

15. Postmaster. It paid very little, but it gave Lincoln access to newspapers.

16. Less than $300 in three years.

17. In Samuel Hill's dry goods store, in New Salem.

18. What other job did Lincoln have while acting as postmaster?
19. How did Lincoln learn the science of surveying?
20. How much money did Lincoln earn while surveying?
21. What are some of the towns Lincoln surveyed?
22. How did Lincoln use his surveying job to benefit himself politically?
23. What happened to Lincoln's horse and surveying equipment in late 1834?
24. Who got Lincoln's surveying equipment back for him?
25. While living in New Salem, what did Lincoln refer to as "the national debt"?
26. What type of work did Lincoln do in the summer of 1835, after his first session in the legislature?
27. What was the name of the town in which Lincoln first owned real estate?
28. On March 16, 1836, Lincoln purchased how many acres of land about a mile east of Huron?
29. How much did he pay for this land?
30. How much did he sell it for?
31. What property did Lincoln buy in his second land speculation?
32. When did Lincoln move from New Salem to Springfield?
33. How long did Lincoln live in New Salem?

18. Deputy county surveyor, working for the county surveyor, John Calhoun. Although Calhoun was a Democrat, it apparently did not bother him to have a Whig working for him.

19. By reading books, such as Robert Gibson's *Treatise on Practical Surveying*. He acquired a compass and chain, a horse, and "went at it."

20. $200 for each quarter section surveyed.

21. Lincoln laid out the towns of Boston, Bath, Petersburg, and Huron.

22. By traveling to different parts of the region, he became more well known outside of his home district. On one survey trip, he purportedly stopped briefly to help harvest wheat in order to win votes.

23. The sheriff confiscated them to pay for notes due on the Lincoln and Berry store.

24. James Short. He bought the equipment for $120 at the sheriff's auction and gave it back to him.

25. The banknotes he owed on the failed Lincoln and Berry store. It took him 15 years to pay off.

26. He continued as postmaster for New Salem, started surveying again, and studied law.

27. Huron. In the spring of 1836 he surveyed Huron, located about 12 miles north of New Salem, and received several lots for his services.

28. Forty-seven. This was his first land speculation.

29. $1.25 per acre, total of $58.75.

30. $80. He sold a half interest in it in 1837 for $30, and split $100 with Dr. Gershom Jayne when they sold the property for $100 in 1848.

31. Two lots in Springfield. He paid $25 each for lots numbers 6 and 8 on Jefferson Street, and later sold them for at least $75.

32. On April 15, 1837.

33. Nearly six years.

⛴ Blackhawk War

1. What was the Black Hawk War and how was Lincoln involved in it?
2. What rank did Lincoln hold in the Blackhawk War?
3. How many men did Lincoln command?
4. Who was Lincoln's first sergeant?
5. While captain, what event resulted in Lincoln's being punished by having to carry a wooden sword for two days?
6. Whose life did Captain Lincoln save while in the militia?
7. While the militia were encamped at Beardstown, Lincoln lost a wrestling match to whom?
8. How long was Lincoln a captain of militia?
9. When Lincoln rejoined the militia the second time as a private, what was the name of the Regular Army officer that mustered him in?
10. How much was Lincoln paid for his service in the Black Hawk War?
11. Where was the land in Iowa?
12. Did Lincoln ever see this land?

✍ Blackhawk War (Answers)

1. In the spring of 1832, Chief Black Hawk and five hundred Sauk and Fox Indian warriors returned to Illinois to reclaim their tribal homeland in northwest Illinois. Lincoln joined a militia unit to help evict them.

2. He was elected captain of his company, the 4th Illinois Volunteers, by the men. This was an accomplishment that, according to a statement by him years later, "gave me more pleasure than anything up to then or since."

3. Over 60.

4. Jack Armstrong.

5. His men stole liquor from the officers' quarters and got so drunk they couldn't march the next day.

6. An old drunken Indian's that stumbled into camp. Some of his men wanted to kill him, but Lincoln protected him.

7. Fellow militiaman Lorenzo D. Thompson.

8. Thirty days. After serving as a captain, he re-enlisted two more times as a private.

9. Second Lieutenant Robert Anderson, who would one day command the Federal forces at Fort Sumter.

10. $125 plus 160 acres of land in Iowa.

11. Forty acres in Tama County and 120 acres in Crawford County.

12. No. He held possession for the rest of his life, however, and his son Robert sold it for $1,800 after his father died.

🏳 Romance

1. Whom did Lincoln fall in love with in 1835?
2. What did Ann look like?
3. To whom was Ann Rutledge engaged when Lincoln first developed an interest in her?
4. What happened to Ann Rutledge?
5. Who was Mary Owens?
6. How did Lincoln meet Mary Owens?
7. Why did Lincoln, who considered Mary Owens unattractive and "weather-beaten," propose marriage to her?
8. Who broke off the engagement between Lincoln and Mary Owens?
9. What was the name of the woman that Lincoln fell in love with after he began courting Mary Todd?
10. Who else was interested in Matilda Edwards?
11. Did Matilda return Lincoln's romantic interests?

✍ Romance (Answers)

1. Ann Rutledge, 22-year-old daughter of New Salem tavern keeper James Rutledge. For years it has been debated whether or not Lincoln was romantically involved with Ann, but historians today generally accept this as true.

2. She had auburn hair, blue eyes, was about five feet, three inches tall and weighed between 120 and 130 pounds.

3. John McNamara (alias John McNeil), who had moved back east with a promise to return and marry Ann. She finally broke off the engagement, and Lincoln and she became serious about each other.

4. She died of "brain fever," which was probably typhoid, on August 25, 1835. Lincoln was extremely despondent over Ann's death.

5. A young lady to whom Lincoln proposed marriage in the fall of 1837. She was originally from Green County, Kentucky.

6. When she visited her sister, Mrs. Abell, in 1833. In the autumn of 1836 Lincoln suggested that if Mrs. Abell would bring her sister back, he would marry her.

7. He felt honor-bound to do so because he had originally suggested it and Mrs. Abell acted upon this suggestion.

8. Mary. She said she found Lincoln "deficient in those little links which make up the chain of a woman's happiness."

9. Matilda Edwards, Mary's cousin.

10. Lincoln's best friend, Joshua Speed.

11. No. She rejected both Lincoln and Speed.

⛁ Legislature

1. Who convinced Lincoln he should run for the state legislature?
2. How old was Lincoln when he first ran for the state legislature?
3. Where was Lincoln's first campaign speech?
4. How did Lincoln describe his politics in his first campaign speech?
5. How well did Lincoln do in his first campaign?
6. What political party did Lincoln identify himself with in his second campaign for the legislature?
7. How well did Lincoln do in his second campaign for the legislature?
8. How did Lincoln get the money to buy a new suit of clothes for his job as a legislator?
9. What material was Lincoln's new suit made of?
10. When did Lincoln's first session of the legislature start?
11. Where did Lincoln live while attending the legislature in Vandalia?
12. How many legislators, besides Lincoln, were freshmen his first year?
13. What was Lincoln's initial salary as a state legislator?
14. How many terms did Lincoln serve in the state legislature?
15. What was the "Long Nine"?
16. What were two of Lincoln's most noteworthy accomplishments while in the state legislature?

✍ Legislature (Answers)

1. Justice of the Peace Bowling Green and the president of the New Salem debating society, James Rutledge.

2. Twenty-two.

3. In Pappsville, Illinois. Lincoln had to interrupt his speech to join in a fight on the side of a friend, Row Herndon. Lincoln threw Herndon's assailant 12 feet through the air and then returned to make his speech.

4. "Short and sweet, like the old woman's dance." During the campaign he described himself as a "Clay" man (meaning Henry Clay, a Whig), as opposed to an Andrew Jackson man, a Democrat.

5. He lost, running 8th in a field of 13 candidates, the top 4 of which went to the legislature. He acquired 277 out of 300 votes in his home district, but lost because of scarcity of votes in other precincts (his total was 657). He would later boast that this was the only time he was defeated "by a direct vote of the people."

6. Neither. Although a Whig, Lincoln received the support of both Democrats and Whigs in his second campaign.

7. He won. He was second in a field of 13 candidates, receiving a total of 1,376 votes.

8. He borrowed $200 from Coleman Smoot, a well-to-do friend. He paid $60 for the new suit and used the rest to pay expenses while he waited for his salary to begin.

9. Blue jeans.

10. It went from December 1, 1834, to February 13, 1835.

11. At a local boarding tavern. He roomed with Whig leader John T. Stuart.

12. Thirty-six out of 55. He was the second youngest of all legislators.

13. $3 per day. This was increased to $4 per day in a subsequent session.

14. Four, from 1834 to 1842.

15. The nine representatives from Sangamon County to the 1836–1837 session of the Illinois State Legislature. The Long Nine consisted of two senators and seven representatives that were all at least six feet in height.

16. Lincoln was instrumental in moving the state capital from Vandalia to Springfield, and in the passage of a statewide internal improvements bill.

17. What kind of leadership role did Lincoln fill while in the legislature?

18. When did Lincoln first speak out publicly against slavery?

19. Who was the other legislator that signed the March 3 protest against slavery with Lincoln?

20. Why did Lincoln jump out of a window during a session of the state legislature in December of 1840?

17. He was de facto floor leader for the Whigs, and served on many committees. He lost both times he tried to become the Speaker of the House.

18. In the state legislature in Vandalia, on March 3, 1837.

19. Daniel Stone.

20. Lincoln and one or two other Whig representatives were trying to prevent a quorum and consequent vote on the State Bank. When the sergeant at arms locked the door and refused to let them leave, they jumped out the second story church window where the legislature was temporarily meeting.

ᛞ Mary Todd Lincoln

1. When was Mary Todd born?
2. Who were Mary's parents?
3. Where did Mary go to school?
4. How many brothers and sisters did Mary have?
5. What did Mary look like?
6. Did Mary ever own slaves?
7. What happened to Mary's mother?
8. Why did Mary leave Lexington?
9. To whom was Mary's sister Elizabeth married?
10. When did Mary first meet Lincoln?
11. Did Ninian and Elizabeth Edwards initially approve of Mary's romance with Lincoln?
12. Was Mary popular with the men of Springfield?
13. What were Lincoln's and Mary's mutual interests?
14. When did Lincoln and Mary get engaged?
15. What other rising politician courted Mary besides Lincoln?
16. Why did Lincoln break off his engagement with Mary in January 1841?
17. How long were Lincoln and Mary separated?
18. Who brought them back together?

✍ Mary Todd Lincoln (Answers)

1. December 13, 1818.
2. Eliza Parker Todd and Robert S. Todd of Lexington, Kentucky. Mary's father was a prosperous merchant, lawyer, banker, and slave owner.
3. At Dr. John Ward's academy and the select boarding school of Madame Victorie Mentelle.
4. Five brothers and sisters, plus eight half brothers and half sisters.
5. She was five feet, two inches tall, with fair skin, light chestnut hair, and blue eyes.
6. No. Her father had slaves, however, and Mary grew up accustomed to the company of house servants.
7. She died when Mary was six years old.
8. She did not get along well with her stepmother, Elizabeth Humphreys Todd. At the age of 21 she decided to go live with her older sister, Elizabeth Edwards, in Springfield in 1839.
9. Ninian Edwards, son of a former governor of Illinois. The Edwardses were among Springfield's social elite, and when Mary came to live with them made certain that all of the town's eligible bachelors came to parties held in her honor.
10. In August 1839.
11. No. They considered Lincoln "pretty rough" and thought of him as her social inferior.
12. Yes. Mary was witty, cultured, an excellent conversationalist, and loved to dance. But she was somewhat haughty and aristocratic at times, and had a mercurial temper.
13. They were both Kentuckians by birth, Whigs in politics, and loved the poetry of Robert Burns. Lincoln was comfortable with Mary because she did most of the talking, and he was normally tongue-tied around women.
14. No definite date is known. Probably in December of 1840.
15. Stephen A. Douglas.
16. He told her he didn't love her. This may have been because he developed a romantic interest in Mary's cousin Matilda Edwards.
17. For over a year. They finally started seeing each other, secretly at first, in the summer of 1842.
18. Mrs. Simeon Francis, wife of the editor of Springfield's Whig organ, the Sangamo *Journal*. They met at the Francises' house.

19. What political project did Lincoln and Mary undertake soon after getting back together?
20. What happened as a result of Lincoln's writing of the anonymous letters about Shields?
21. What happened at Lincoln's duel?
22. When Lincoln's future law partner Herndon first met Mary Todd in 1837 he said something to her that she took as an insult, never forgiving him. What did he say?
23. When and where were Lincoln and Mary married?
24. Who married them?
25. What was engraved on Mary's wedding ring?
26. What were some of Lincoln's nicknames for Mary?
27. How many of Mary's sisters lived in Springfield?
28. What financial aid did Mary's father provide her?
29. How much did Mary receive from the estate of her father when he died in 1849?
30. Once, when Lincoln was traveling on the Eighth Circuit, Mary asked another man to come stay with her and her son Bob. Whom did she ask and why?
31. When Tad was an infant, Mary breastfed not only him but another baby for a while. Whose other child did she nurse?

19. They started writing a series of anonymous letters in the Sangamo *Journal* making fun of State Auditor James Shields.
20. Shields challenged Lincoln to a duel. Lincoln accepted.
21. Lincoln selected cavalry broadswords as weapons, which would have given him a tremendous advantage, as Shields was a small man. But friends intervened and prevented the duel from happening.
22. Herndon and Mary had danced a waltz, and, intending to compliment her, he told her she "seemed to glide through the waltz with the ease of a serpent."
23. On November 4, 1842, in the parlor of Ninian and Matilda Edwards.
24. They were married by Episcopalian Minister Charles Dresser.
25. "Love is eternal."
26. Molly, Puss, Little Woman, Child Wife, and Mother.
27. Three. Elizabeth, Frances, and Anne.
28. He provided Mary with $120/year stipend and deeded them an 80-acre tract of land in Illinois.
29. Approximately $1,000. He died without a will, and the estate was divided between his widow and 14 children.
30. A neighbor, James Gourley. Mary had found out her maid was sneaking a boyfriend into the maids' room at night, which frightened her. Gourley was a trusted friend she sought for her and the children's protection.
31. Mrs. Charles Dallman's. Mrs. Dallman was sick and unable to nurse her own infant.

♻ Springfield

1. Who was Lincoln's best friend, in the late 1830s?
2. Where did Lincoln live when he first moved to Springfield?
3. Where did the Lincolns first live after marrying?
4. How much did the Lincolns pay to live in the Globe Tavern?
5. Where did the Lincolns move after Robert was born?
6. To where did the Lincolns move in May 1844?
7. From whom did they buy their house, and how much did they pay?
8. What significant enhancement to the transportation system of Sangamon County occurred in July 1849?
9. What was the population of Springfield in 1850?
10. How much did Lincoln typically pay for firewood in the 1850s?
11. Where did he purchase his firewood?
12. What was the name of the bank the Lincolns used in the 1850s?
13. What was the name of the black laundress that worked part time for the Lincolns in the early 1850s?
14. Who was Lincoln's barber in Springfield?
15. In the fall of 1854 the Lincolns sold the 80 acres Mary's father had given them in Sangamon County. How much did they get for it?
16. What changes did the Lincolns make to their house in April 1856?
17. What was the name of the contractors that did the remodeling of the Lincoln house?
18. Into what style and color did Mary transform the house?
19. How many rooms did the Lincoln home have after remodeling?

✍ Springfield (Answers)

1. Joshua Speed.
2. He moved in with Joshua Speed, above Speed's Dry Goods store.
3. In the Globe Tavern, a boarding house, on the north side of Adams Street, between Third and Fourth Streets.
4. Room and board was $4 per week for an 8-foot by 14-foot room. They ate in the common dining room on the first floor.
5. They rented a three-room frame house at 214 South Fourth Street.
6. They bought their first and only house at the corner of Eighth and Jackson Streets in Springfield.
7. Reverend Charles Dresser, the minister that had married them. They paid $1,200 plus a lot they owned on Adams Street, valued at $300.
8. The railroad.
9. Approximately 5,000 people, about 170 of which were free blacks.
10. $4 per cord.
11. From local dry goods merchants, such as C. M. & S. Smith.
12. The Springfield Marine and Fire Insurance Company.
13. Mariah Vance. She also occasionally helped with the cooking.
14. William Florville, "Willy the barber."
15. $1,200.
16. They raised the roof, creating a full second story. Mary did this while Lincoln was traveling on the Eighth Judicial Circuit, but probably had his concurrence beforehand.
17. Hammon and Ragsdale.
18. Greek Revival, chocolate brown with green shutters.
19. Five rooms downstairs and five rooms, plus a "trunk" room, upstairs.

♔ Congressman Lincoln

1. When Lincoln became interested in Congress, he and two other Whig politicians decided to take turns running for the Seventh Congressional District, each to fill a single, successive turn. Who were the other politicians?

2. What happened when Lincoln's turn for Congress came?

3. Who was his Democratic opponent in Lincoln's congressional race of 1846?

4. What did Cartwright claim about Lincoln in his effort to discredit him during the campaign?

5. What was the result of the election?

6. Joshua Speed and several Whig leaders banded together to provide Lincoln $200 for his expenses during his campaign against Cartwright. How much of this did Lincoln spend?

7. How much time elapsed between Lincoln's election to Congress and when he actually took office?

8. Of which Congress was Lincoln a member?

9. Where did the Lincolns live while in Washington?

10. What recreation did Lincoln engage in while living in Washington?

11. How large of a population did Washington have when Lincoln was a member of the House of Representatives?

12. What association did Lincoln have with the Washington Monument while in Congress?

13. Why did Mary leave Washington and take the children to Lexington, Kentucky, while Lincoln was in Congress?

14. How many roll calls did Lincoln answer during his two-year term in the House of Representatives?

15. What committees was Lincoln a member of while in Congress?

16. Who was the most famous member of the House during Lincoln's term?

17. What southern Whig congressman did Lincoln develop a respect for while in Washington?

✍ Congressman Lincoln (Answers)

1. James Hardin and Edward D. Baker.

2. Lincoln was to go third, after James Hardin and Edward D. Baker. Hardin, who had gone first, decided he wanted to have a second term and tried to outmaneuver Lincoln from the nomination. But Lincoln successfully obtained the Whig Party nomination and ran for office.

3. Peter Cartwright, the famous Methodist circuit rider and evangelist.

4. That Lincoln, who was not a member of any Christian church, was an "infidel." Lincoln decided to publish a handbill explaining his religious beliefs and refute Cartwright's claim.

5. Lincoln won. He defeated Cartwright by an unprecedented majority of 56 percent of the 11,418 votes cast.

6. Seventy-five cents. This was for a barrel of cider, "which some farmhands insisted I treat them to." He returned the rest to Joshua Speed.

7. Over a year. He was elected on August 3, 1846, and took office in December 1847.

8. The 30th.

9. The boardinghouse of Mrs. Ann G. Sprigg, east of the Capitol on land now occupied by the Library of Congress.

10. Bowling at lanes owned by James Casparis.

11. Forty thousand people, including two thousand slaves.

12. He took part in the laying of the cornerstone and the dedication ceremonies.

13. Mary and the boys were not comfortable at the boardinghouse, and she didn't get along well with some of the guests. She went to live with her father in Lexington, Kentucky.

14. Four hundred forty-three out of 456 possible.

15. Committee on Expenditures in the War Department and Committee on Post Offices and Post Roads.

16. John Quincy Adams, who died early in the first session.

17. Alexander Stephens of Georgia, the future vice president of the Confederate States of America.

18. On what hot political issue did Congressman Lincoln attack democratic President Polk?

19. What were the "spot resolutions"?

20. What was the political reaction to Lincoln's spot resolutions?

21. Why did Lincoln serve only one term in Congress?

22. Who, in the Thirtieth Congress were the "Young Indians"?

23. Whom did Lincoln support as presidential candidate in 1848?

24. How many other Whigs did Illinois send to the House of Representatives during Lincoln's term in Congress?

25. What was Lincoln's position on slavery when he was in Congress?

26. What did Lincoln try to do about slavery while he was in Congress?

27. What was Lincoln's salary while in Congress?

28. Who was the next Seventh Congressional District Whig nominee after Lincoln left office?

29. What appointed political office did Lincoln try to obtain for himself after he left Congress?

30. Did Lincoln get the appointment as commissioner of the General Land Office?

31. What other political appointments did the secretary of the interior offer to Lincoln as a consolation to his loss of the General Land Office?

18. He demanded to know whether or not America had actually started the war with Mexico or had been a victim of Mexican aggression, as the Polk administration claimed.

19. A series of resolutions introduced by Lincoln in Congress that required President Polk to provide Congress with evidence that the initial battles of the Mexican War were actually on Mexican, rather than Texas, soil.

20. Congress and the president ignored them, but Lincoln's constituents back in the Seventh Congressional District disapproved of them. He became the object of a great deal of political derision, with the democratic press claiming falsely he was not supporting the troops in Mexico.

21. Like his predecessors, Hardin and Baker, he had pledged to serve only one term. So he didn't even try to be re-elected. Even if he had, however, it may have been difficult because of the effect of his spot resolutions.

22. Lincoln, Alexander H. Stephens, and a small group of other Whigs in the House of Representatives that opposed the Mexican War and sought political reform in the Whig Party.

23. Mexican war hero and Whig candidate General Zachary Taylor.

24. Zero. Lincoln was the only Whig from Illinois.

25. He opposed slavery, and voted for the Wilmot Proviso, which prohibited slavery in the territories captured in the Mexican War, at least five times.

26. He proposed a bill to ban slavery in the District of Columbia, but was not able to muster enough support to get it formally submitted to the House.

27. $8 per day.

28. Stephen T. Logan. Logan was defeated by his democratic opponent.

29. Commissioner of the General Land Office.

30. No. The Taylor administration gave it to Justin Butterfield instead.

31. First, the office of secretary to the governor of the Oregon Territory, and then the office of the governor itself. Lincoln turned both down, realizing they were political dead ends.

♫ Religious Beliefs

1. What church did Thomas and Nancy Lincoln attend in Kentucky?

2. How were the Separate Baptists different from other Baptists of the region?

3. What church did the Lincolns attend in Indiana?

4. What was peculiar about the beliefs of the Pigeon Creek Baptists?

5. What was Lincoln's job at the Pigeon Creek Baptist Church?

6. What two books did Lincoln read while in New Salem that were considered heretical by his more orthodox Christian friends?

7. Lincoln later said he was never a skeptic of Christianity, but that he had argued in favor of the "Doctrine of Necessity." What is the Doctrine of Necessity?

8. To what church did Lincoln belong?

9. Where did the Lincolns go to church in Springfield?

10. What did the Lincolns pay to rent a pew in the First Presbyterian Church?

11. What church did Lincoln attend in Washington?

12. What book did Lincoln say was "the best book God has given to man"?

13. While in the White House, what books of the Bible did Lincoln read the most?

14. Was Abraham Lincoln an atheist?

15. Was Abraham Lincoln a Christian?

✍ Religious Beliefs (Answers)

1. The Little Mount Separate Baptist.

2. They accepted no creed except the Bible itself and were vocally antislavery.

3. Pigeon Creek Baptist.

4. They were called "hard shell" Baptists, and had strong Calvinist leanings that believed only those predestined by God would be saved.

5. Sexton. He cleaned up the building and was responsible for small jobs such as furnishing it with candles.

6. Thomas Paine's *Age of Reason* and Constantin de Volney's *Ruins of Civilizations*.

7. Basically, the Doctrine of Necessity is fatalism. Lincoln described it as "the human mind is impelled to action or held in rest by some power, over which the mind itself has no control."

8. Lincoln never joined a church. He once said that "When any church shall inscribe over its altar, as its sole qualification for membership, the Saviour's condensed statement of the substance of both Law and Gospel, 'Thou shalt love the Lord thy God with all thy heart, and with all thy soul, and with all thy mind, and thy neighbor as thyself,' that church will I join with all my heart and all my soul."

9. Prior to 1852, Mary attended St. Paul's Episcopal Church. In 1852, after Eddie died, Mary and Lincoln attended the First Presbyterian Church. Mary joined, but Lincoln did not.

10. Between $25 to $50 a year.

11. They attended the New York Avenue Presbyterian Church fairly regularly, but did not join.

12. The Bible.

13. Psalms and the Old Testament prophets.

14. No. There is no conclusive evidence that Lincoln ever doubted the existence of God.

15. There is no conclusive evidence that Lincoln personally accepted Christ. He did, however, believe that Jesus was the "Savior."

Sons

1. What was the name and birth date of the Lincolns' first child?
2. What was the name and birth date of the Lincolns' second child?
3. What was the name and birth date of the Lincolns' third child?
4. What was the name and birth date of the Lincolns' fourth child?
5. Which of the Lincoln children most closely resembled his father in his personality traits?
6. When and from what cause did the Lincolns' second son, Eddie, die?
7. What was Thomas' nickname?
8. What physical disability did Tad have?
9. How would Lincoln transport his children around town when they were small?
10. What trick did Lincoln's sons and neighborhood children enjoy playing on Lincoln when they saw him coming home for supper?
11. What learning delays did Tad have?
12. What were the names of Willie and Tad's closest friends in Washington?
13. What was the name of the Taft boys' 16-year-old sister that supervised them?
14. What was Lincoln's nickname for Julia?
15. Whose tragic death on February 20, 1862, plunged Mary and Lincoln into mourning?
16. What was the cause of Willie's death?
17. Who else came down with typhoid fever?
18. When Tad was getting close to recovering from his fever, one day he refused to take his medicine, and the nurse asked Lincoln to help convince him to take it. How did Lincoln get Tad to take his medicine?
19. After Willie's death, whom did Tad become close to?

✍ Sons (Answers)

1. Robert Todd Lincoln was born on August 1, 1843.
2. Edward, born on March 10, 1846. Eddie was named after Lincoln's friend and political associate, Edward D. Baker.
3. William Wallace, who was called Willie, was born on December 21, 1850.
4. Thomas, born on April 4, 1853. Thomas was named after Lincoln's father.
5. Willie.
6. Eddie died on February 1, 1850, from pulmonary tuberculosis.
7. Tad. Lincoln called his son this when an infant, because he had such a large head. He said he looked like a tadpole.
8. Tad had a cleft palate and a bad lisp.
9. By either pulling them in a wagon or putting them up on his shoulders.
10. They liked to try to knock off his hat, and then jump on him.
11. At the age of nine, he still could not read or write.
12. Horatio N. Taft (known as "Bud") and Halsey Cook Taft (known as "Holly"), sons of a federal judge who lived nearby. They were approximately the same ages as the Lincoln boys.
13. Julia.
14. Flibbertygibbet. Lincoln described a flibbertygibbet as "a small slim thing with curls and a white dress and blue sash that flies instead of walking."
15. Their son Willie's.
16. It was called "bilious fever," which was probably typhoid fever.
17. Tad, but his health improved.
18. He wrote him a check for $5.
19. His father. Lincoln played with him as much as possible, and Tad usually slept in his father's bed.

20. What did Lincoln telegraph to Mary on June 9, 1862, who was visiting Philadelphia, after having a bad dream about Tad?

21. Where did Robert Lincoln go to school as a teenager?

22. What happened when Robert took the entrance exams for Harvard College?

23. What nickname was given to Robert Lincoln after his father was nominated for president?

24. What did Robert Lincoln do after graduating from Harvard in late 1864?

25. What did Robert do in the army?

26. How did he get the position on Grant's staff?

27. Did Robert Lincoln ever marry?

20. He asked her to put Tad's toy pistol away.
21. Illinois State University in Springfield—which was actually a local preparatory school.
22. He failed, and had to attend Phillips Exeter Academy in New Hampshire to get ready for Harvard.
23. Prince of Rails.
24. He enlisted in the army.
25. He was a captain on General Grant's staff.
26. Lincoln, in trying to calm Mary's fears about harm coming to Robert, asked Grant if he would take him onto his personal staff at "some nominal rank." Lincoln even offered to pay Robert's salary.
27. Yes. He married Mary Harlan, daughter of Senator James Harlan, on September 24, 1868.

⚑ Early Law Career

1. With what book did Lincoln start his study of the law while in New Salem?

2. What other books, besides *Blackstone's Commentaries*, did Lincoln study in preparation for the bar?

3. What inspired Lincoln to study law?

4. Where did Lincoln get most of his law books?

5. When was Lincoln admitted to the Sangamon Bar?

6. Who was Lincoln's first law partner?

7. What percentage of the fees of Stuart and Lincoln did Lincoln receive?

8. Who was Lincoln's second law partner?

9. What percentage of the fees of Logan and Lincoln did Lincoln receive?

10. Where in Springfield was the Logan and Lincoln law office located?

11. What young man studied law under Logan and Lincoln?

12. Why did Logan, the Sangamon Bar's most respected attorney, choose the relatively inexperienced Lincoln as a law partner?

13. Why and when did Logan and Lincoln dissolve their partnership?

✍ Early Law Career (Answers)

1. *Blackstone's Commentaries.* He acquired a copy while visiting Springfield, and began studying law on his own.

2. Chitty's *Pleadings* and Greenleaf's *Evidence.*

3. He was a juror on three small civil cases, and between this and the encouragement of the Justice of the Peace Bowling Green, he decided that he could become a successful lawyer, even without formal education.

4. He borrowed them from attorney John T. Stuart.

5. March 1, 1837.

6. John T. Stuart, who had roomed with Lincoln while they were legislators in Vandalia.

7. Fifty.

8. Stephen T. Logan, one of the most capable lawyers in the state.

9. Thirty-three.

10. In the third floor of the Tinsley Building, right above the United States District Court on the southwest corner of 6th and Adams Streets.

11. William Herndon, who would later become Lincoln's junior partner.

12. Logan was a skilled lawyer but a poor public speaker. He said he thought that Lincoln, with his excellent public speaking abilities, would be "exceedingly useful to me in getting the good will of juries."

13. In the fall of 1844, because Logan wanted to bring his son, David, into the partnership.

🏳 Pets

1. How did Lincoln treat animals?
2. While the Thomas Lincoln family was in transit from Indiana to Illinois, what accident nearly killed Lincoln's dog?
3. What pets did Lincoln particularly enjoy playing with when he lived in New Salem?
4. What was the name of the horse Lincoln rode in his early years on the Eighth Judicial Circuit?
5. What was the name of the horse Lincoln rode in his later years on the Eighth Judicial Circuit?
6. What was the name of the dog that Willie and Tad had to leave in Springfield when the Lincolns moved to the White House?
7. Who kept Fido when the Lincolns moved away?
8. What was the name of Lincoln's horse that was left behind in Springfield?
9. What were the names of Willie and Tad's two goats they had while in the White House?
10. What stunt did Tad and Nanko perform one day in the East Room of the White House?
11. What kind of trouble did the goats frequently get into around the White House?
12. What happened to Tad's goat, Nanny?
13. What was the name of Tad's dog that liked to sit next to Lincoln in the White House while he was eating and beg for scraps?
14. What was the name of the pet turkey that Tad managed to save from becoming the 1863 Thanksgiving dinner at the White House?
15. What tragic accident caused the death of Tad and Willie's ponies on February 10, 1864?
16. Who was arrested for starting the stable fire?

🖋 Pets (Answers)

1. Very kindly. He would scold other children if he saw them mistreating animals, and once said that "an ant's life was to it as sweet as our own."

2. The dog jumped out of the wagon and broke through the ice. Lincoln had to go through icecold, waist deep water to rescue him.

3. Kittens.

4. Old Tom.

5. Old Buck.

6. Fido.

7. Two neighbor boys, John and Frank Roll.

8. Old Bob.

9. Nanko and Nanny.

10. Tad harnessed Nanko to a chair and had the goat pull him through the East Room while a reception was in progress.

11. They frequently got into trouble with the gardener, eating flowers and ornamentals.

12. She disappeared when Tad and his mother were on a trip to Philadelphia. The gardener may have had something to do with this.

13. Jip.

14. Jack.

15. The White House stable burned down. Lincoln tried to rescue the ponies and horses, but the fire had progressed too far before he got there.

16. Lincoln's coachman, Patterson McGee.

Herndon and Lincoln's Law Practice

1. When Lincoln decided to begin his own law firm, whom did he take as his partner?
2. How did Lincoln and Herndon split their fees?
3. Why did Lincoln select Herndon as his law partner?
4. What were some of Herndon's personal traits and characteristics?
5. Where was the Lincoln and Herndon law office located?
6. How much did Herndon spend to furnish their law office, when they first set it up?
7. What fees did Lincoln and Herndon typically charge their clients?
8. How large was the Eighth Judicial Circuit in 1843?
9. How often did Lincoln travel the circuit?
10. How long did it take to complete the circuit?
11. What was Lincoln's average annual income from his law practice in the 1840s?
12. Who was the first Judge Lincoln traveled with on the Eighth Judicial Circuit?
13. What was the name of the man, who later became a good friend of Lincoln's, who replaced Treat as circuit judge?
14. Who occasionally substituted as judge for David Davis on the Eighth Judicial Circuit?
15. How many Illinois counties encompassed the Eighth Judicial Circuit in the early 1850s?
16. With whom did Lincoln form a second law partnership in 1852?
17. What was the major complaint other lawyers of the Eighth Judicial Circuit had about Lincoln?
18. What succinct advice did Lincoln offer to young men considering the law as a profession?
19. What was Lincoln's annual income from his law practice in the early 1850s?

✍ Herndon and Lincoln's Law Practice (Answers)

1. William H. Herndon, who would remain his partner for the rest of Lincoln's life.
2. 50-50, in spite of the fact Herndon was the junior partner. Herndon kept the books, and usually just divided up the cash received with Lincoln.
3. He liked Herndon and thought him a good student of the law. He also believed he would benefit him politically, by providing a connection with the young Whigs of the town.
4. Quick, upbeat, well read, and a sharp dresser. But he lacked a sense of humor.
5. In the Tinsley Building, like the Lincoln and Logan office had been.
6. $168.65 for furniture and miscellaneous furnishings.
7. $5 for an appearance before the justice of the peace, $10 to $25 in circuit court, and up to $100 for the Illinois Supreme Court.
8. It encompassed over 10,000 square miles and 14 counties.
9. Twice a year, usually from mid-March to mid-June, and then from early September to early December.
10. At least 10 weeks.
11. Between $1,500 and $2,000.
12. Samuel H. Treat.
13. David Davis.
14. Lincoln.
15. Eleven. They were Tazwell, Woodford, McLean, Logan, DeWitt, Piatt, Champaign, Vermillion, Edgar, Macon, and Christian.
16. In Vermillion County he and a local lawyer by the name of Ward Lamon formed the partnership of Lincoln and Lamon. The formation of this partnership was probably Lamon's idea, and it did not impact the Lincoln and Herndon relationship.
17. They complained that his fees were too low. They once held a mock "trial," Judge Davis presiding, in which Lincoln was accused of the crime of charging fees that were too small.
18. He told them to "resolve to be honest at all events; and if in your own judgment you cannot be an honest lawyer, resolve to be honest without being a lawyer. Choose some other occupation, rather than one in the choosing of which you do, in advance, consent to be a knave."
19. About $2,000 per year.

20. In the years 1849–1850, Lincoln frequently stayed out on the circuit for weeks at a time, refusing to come home on the weekends like the other layers. Why did he do this?

21. In the mid-1850s, Lincoln's law practice became increasingly involved with what industry?

22. In early 1856 Lincoln won a major court case for the Illinois Central Railroad, earning his largest fee up to that time. How much did he earn?

23. What were the facts involved in the Hurd vs. Rock Island Bridge Company case (also known as the *Effie Afton* case)?

24. What was the result of Lincoln's efforts in the *Effie Afton* Case?

25. What Chicago law firm did Lincoln briefly consider joining?

26. What well-known Pittsburgh lawyer would become co-counsel with Lincoln in the famous McCormick Reaper lawsuit?

27. During the McCormick Reaper case, Stanton ignored Lincoln's counsel and called him what insulting name?

28. How much did Lincoln earn in the McCormick Reaper case?

29. What year was Lincoln's most profitable as a lawyer?

30. In his celebrated court case of 1859, how did Lincoln prove the innocence of Duff Armstrong, who supposedly had been seen committing murder in the light of the full moon?

31. What was the name of the man Duff had been accused of murdering?

32. Where did the murder take place?

33. How was Lincoln associated with Duff Armstrong?

34. How much did Lincoln receive in legal fees for defending Duff Armstrong?

35. What was the name of the witness Lincoln discredited with the Almanac?

20. He and Mary did not get along well.
21. Railroading. Lincoln became known as a railroad lawyer.
22. $5,000. But he had to sue his client to get the money. It involved a civil suit regarding McLean County's efforts to tax the railroad.
23. The steamer *Effie Afton* ran into one of the piers of the first railroad bridge across the Mississippi River. The *Effie Afton's* owner, John S. Hurd, claimed the bridge was an obstruction to river traffic.
24. Lincoln proved the *Effie Afton* crashed because the starboard engine failed, resulting in a hung jury, dismissal of the case, and victory for Lincoln and the railroads.
25. Grant Goodrich's.
26. Edwin M. Stanton, a brilliant lawyer that would one day be Lincoln's secretary of war.
27. A long-armed ape.
28. $1,400. He tried to return $1,000 of it because his counsel was not accepted, but the senior counsel insisted he keep it.
29. 1857. He earned more that year in legal fees than any other.
30. He used a Farmer's Almanac to prove that the moon had already set at the time of the murder.
31. James Preston Metzker. Metzker had been attending a religious camp meeting.
32. At Virgin's Grove, near New Salem.
33. Duff was the son of Jack Armstrong, whom Lincoln had wrestled and befriended when first coming to New Salem.
34. Nothing. He did not ask for any compensation.
35. Charles Allen, who had testified he had seen Duff strike Metzker from 150 feet away in the light of the full moon.

36. How many total appearances did Lincoln make before the Illinois Supreme Court?

37. What did Lincoln do about his law partnership with Herndon when he left for Washington?

36. Over three hundred.

37. He left it intact. He said to Herndon "give our clients to know that the election of a President makes no change in the firm of Lincoln and Herndon. If I live I'm coming back some time, and then we'll go right on practicing law as if nothing ever happened."

🏳 1850s Politics

1. What political leader did Lincoln call his "Beau ideal of a statesman"?
2. Why did Lincoln join the Whig, as opposed to the Democratic Party?
3. What was a "Locofoco"?
4. Whom did Lincoln eulogize in July 1850?
5. In what official capacity did Lincoln serve the Whig Party during the 1852 presidential campaign?
6. Who was the Whig presidential nominee in 1852?
7. Whom did Lincoln eulogize in 1852?
8. What new political party developed largely as a result of the growing dissatisfaction towards the Kansas Nebraska Act?
9. What short-lived political party was organized in the mid-1850s as a result of a dislike of foreigners and Catholics?
10. What Whig congressman did Lincoln campaign for in 1854?
11. Was Lincoln's campaign for Yates successful?
12. What political cause did Lincoln take up while campaigning for Yates, and afterwards continue in his own political battles?
13. What political office was Lincoln elected to in November 1854?
14. Why did Lincoln have mixed emotions about the prospect of returning to the state legislature in 1854?
15. Did Lincoln take his seat in the Illinois State Legislature after being elected in 1854?
16. What political office did Lincoln begin to seek in 1854?
17. How did Lincoln try to gain the US Senate seat in 1855?
18. What happened in the state legislature regarding Lincoln's attempt to win the senate seat in 1855?
19. When did Lincoln join the Republican Party?
20. Where was the Republican Party's first presidential convention and whom did it nominate?

✍ 1850s Politics (Answers)

1. Henry Clay, a leader in the Whig Party.
2. He thought the Whig Party represented economic growth, development, and progress.
3. A Democrat.
4. Zachary Taylor, for the Common Council of Chicago.
5. Whig national committeeman for Illinois.
6. Winfield Scott, military hero of both the War of 1812 and the Mexican War. He was defeated by the Democratic contender, Franklin Pierce.
7. Henry Clay, in Springfield.
8. The Republican Party. It was organized in 1854.
9. The Native American Party. It was also known as the Order of the Star-Spangled Banner and the Know-Nothing Party.
10. Richard Yates, who was seeking re-election in the Seventh Congressional District of Illinois.
11. No. Yates was defeated by his Democratic opponent, Thomas L. Harris.
12. Fighting the Kansas Nebraska Act.
13. A fifth term in the Illinois State Legislature. Sangamon County voters gave him the highest number of votes of any candidate.
14. Because he wanted to seek higher political office.
15. No. He couldn't run for the Senate if he was a member of the legislature, so he declined to take his seat.
16. The US Senate. Lincoln sought support of anti-Nebraska forces for the Whig nomination for the Senate.
17. By lining up votes in the Illinois State Legislature. Prior to 1913, US senators were elected by the state legislature instead of the direct vote of the people.
18. He lost. Although Lincoln started with the highest number of votes in the state senate, he ended up having to throw his support to democrat Lyman Trumbull in order to make certain a pro-slavery candidate didn't win.
19. In the spring of 1856. On May 29, 1856, Lincoln made the closing speech at the convention that founded the Illinois Republican Party in Bloomington, Illinois.
20. In Philadelphia. They nominated John C. Fremont, a well-known explorer.

21. Who was the Republican Party's vice presidential candidate in 1856?

22. Who received the second highest number of votes at the 1856 convention for the vice presidential slot?

23. What did Lincoln say when friends brought him the news that he was almost chosen as Fremont's vice presidential running mate?

24. What was Lincoln's famous "lost speech"?

25. Has the text of the Lost Speech ever been found?

26. What was Lincoln's main theme in the Lost Speech?

27. When Lincoln made his speech accepting the Republican Party's 1858 nomination for the senate, what biblical analogy did Lincoln make regarding the nation and slavery?

28. What other Republican was briefly considered in Lincoln's place for the party's Senate race against Douglas in 1858?

29. Did Lincoln have a campaign manager in his 1858 senate campaign?

30. What did Lincoln say was the "sheet anchor of American republicanism"?

21. William C. Dayton, former senator from New Jersey.

22. Abraham Lincoln, who received 110 votes compared to Dayton's 253.

23. "I reckon that ain't me; there's another great man in Massachusetts named Lincoln, and I reckon it's him."

24. A speech that Lincoln delivered on May 29, 1856, at the conclusion of the Illinois Republican state convention in Bloomington. It supposedly was one of his best speeches, and so captivating that no one bothered to take notes.

25. No. Only a brief synopsis of it was found in the *Alton Courier* of June 5, 1856. A lengthy construction by Henry C. Whitney in 1896 has been discounted by historians.

26. Lincoln stressed that the "Union must be preserved in the purity of its principles as well as the integrity of its territorial parts." He also warned of an increase in the "sentiment in favor of white slavery" in the slave states.

27. "A house divided against itself cannot stand." He believed that the nation could not endure half slave and half free.

28. "Long John" Wentworth, Republican mayor of Chicago. By the time of the Republican convention in Springfield on June 16, however, Lincoln was the only candidate seriously considered.

29. No. He had no designated campaign manager, and no secretarial staff.

30. That no man "is good enough to govern another man without that other's consent."

Stephen A. Douglas and the Debates

1. When did Lincoln and Stephen A. Douglas first meet in political conflict?

2. When did Lincoln and Douglas first meet in formal debate away from the state legislature?

3. What woman did both Lincoln and Douglas court in the late 1830s?

4. When did Lincoln begin publicly arguing with Douglas on the Kansas Nebraska Act?

5. What did Lincoln complain about most in regards to Douglas's attitude towards slavery?

6. What did Douglas say when he heard Lincoln was going to be his opponent for the US Senate in 1858?

7. How many speeches, counting the Lincoln-Douglas debates, did the candidates make during the Senate campaign?

8. Where were the seven Lincoln-Douglas debates held?

9. What was the format of the debates between Douglas and Lincoln?

10. What was unique about the way the press covered the debates?

11. Who were the shorthand experts that recorded the debates, and what newspapers did they represent?

12. Where did Lincoln supposedly utter his famous "you can fool all of the people some of the time, and some of the people all of the time, but you cannot fool all of the people all of the time"?

13. How many people saw the debate at Ottawa?

14. What was the key question Lincoln challenged Douglas to answer regarding slavery in the new territories at the second debate of Freeport?

15. Why did Douglas' response to this question, which became known as the Freeport Doctrine, have so much significance?

16. How many people saw the debate at Freeport?

17. How many people saw the debate at Jonesboro?

✍ Stephen A. Douglas and the Debates (Answers)

1. In the 1836 session of the Illinois State Legislature.

2. On November 19, 1839, Lincoln and three other Whigs debated Douglas and three other Democrats over presidential campaign issues.

3. Mary Todd.

4. September 1854.

5. That Douglas was indifferent as to whether or not it was a moral wrong or right. Whereas Lincoln talked about the "monstrous injustice" of slavery, Douglas considered laws regulating slavery to be of no more importance than the "cranberry laws of Indiana."

6. "I shall have my hands full. He is as honest as he is shrewd; and if I beat him my victory will be hardly won."

7. Douglas, 130; Lincoln, 63.

8. In the Illinois towns of Ottawa, August 21, 1858; Freeport, August 27; Jonesboro, September 15; Charleston, September 18; Galesburg, October 7; Quincy, October 13; and Alton, October 15.

9. The opening speaker was allowed an hour for his presentation, the opponent an hour and a half to reply, and then the initial speaker had a half hour for a rebuttal.

10. Men capable of shorthand took down every word of the debates.

11. Robert R. Hitt of the Republican newspaper Chicago *Press and Tribune*; James B. Sheridan and Henry Binmore for the Democratic paper, the Chicago *Times*.

12. Purportedly, in Clinton, Illinois, on September, 8, 1858, between the second and third debates. That Lincoln actually made this statement has never been accepted by scholars.

13. 10,000.

14. Whether or not the people of any territory could "exclude slavery from its limits prior to the formation of a state constitution."

15. It put Douglas at odds with other Democrats, especially Southerners and President Buchanan, when he answered that people of a territory could, in fact, exclude slavery.

16. Between 12,000 and 15,000.

17. Fewer than two thousand.

18. What did Lincoln say was the fundamental issue of the Senate campaign?
19. What were the results of the Senate race between Douglas and Lincoln?
20. What percentage of the vote did each man receive?
21. What was Lincoln's famous quote about civil liberty he made after losing the Senate race to Douglas?
22. How did Lincoln publicly promote the speeches he had made during his debates with Douglas?
23. What was the last political contest Lincoln and Douglas engaged in?
24. Who stepped forward and offered to hold Lincoln's hat when Lincoln was ready to make his inaugural address?
25. When did Stephen A. Douglas die?
26. What were Douglas' last words of advice to his sons?

18. He believed it was that some men "think slavery a wrong" and others "do not think it a wrong."

19. Douglas won.

20. Neither Lincoln nor Douglas' names appeared on any ballots, so it is not known exactly how many people voted for either man. But republican legislature candidates received about 50 percent of the popular vote, which was not enough, taking into consideration democratic holdovers in the senate, to gain a majority. Consequently, Douglas retained his seat.

21. "The fight must go on. The cause of civil liberty must not be surrendered at the end of one, or even one hundred, defeats."

22. He took his scrapbook of the newspaper reports of the speeches and had them published in a 268-page book titled *Political Debates between Hon. Abraham Lincoln and Hon. Stephen A. Douglas, in the Celebrated Campaign of 1858, in Illinois.*

23. Their campaign for the presidency in 1860.

24. Stephen A. Douglas.

25. June 3, 1861. He died from sickness contrived while traveling across the country, encouraging loyalty to the Union.

26. "Tell them to obey the laws and support the Constitution of the United States."

🏳 Slavery

1. What decision by the US Supreme Court on March 6, 1857, intensified the slavery debate?
2. Who was Dred Scott?
3. Who was chief justice of the Supreme Court in 1857?
4. What did Taney and the Supreme Court rule in the Dred Scott decision?
5. What impact did the Dred Scott decision have on Lincoln?
6. What four individuals did Lincoln say had conspired to nationalize slavery?
7. What radical abolitionist and handful of followers captured the Federal arsenal at Harper's Ferry in October 1859?
8. On what day was John Brown hanged?
9. What did Lincoln believe the underlying cause of the Civil War was?
10. Why didn't Lincoln announce the elimination of slavery as a war aim when he called for the first 75,000 volunteers?
11. What western military commander proclaimed, in August 1861, that the slaves within his department were free?
12. How did Lincoln react to Fremont's order?
13. Whom did Fremont send to Washington, D.C. to argue with Lincoln in favor of his proclamation?
14. What two primary reasons did Lincoln have for revoking the Fremont Proclamation?
15. What was the reaction to Lincoln's revocation of Fremont's order to free the slaves in his department?
16. On November 30, 1861, a man was convicted of importing slaves and sentenced to hang. What was his name?
17. Did Lincoln commute Gordon's death sentence?

✍ Slavery (Answers)

1. The Dred Scott decision.

2. A slave who sued for his freedom. He had traveled with his master from Missouri to Illinois and then the Minnesota Territory, and Scott sued for his freedom when his master died, claiming that his temporary residence in a free state and territory gave him his right to freeman's status.

3. Roger B. Taney of Maryland.

4. That Scott, as a Negro, was not a citizen of the United States and had no right to sue. The Supreme Court also ruled that Congress could not exclude slavery from the territories.

5. Lincoln's faith in the national judiciary was shaken, and he began to espouse the theory that members of the Supreme Court, Congress, and the president were conspiring to spread slavery to all the states.

6. Stephen, Roger, Franklin, and James—meaning Douglas of the Senate, Taney of the Supreme Court, former president Pierce, and current president Buchanan.

7. John Brown.

8. December 2, 1859.

9. Slavery.

10. He considered saving the Union to be the most important thing, and believed that to announce it as a war against slavery would have caused men to refuse to enlist.

11. John C. Fremont. He was commander of the Department of the West, headquartered in St. Louis.

12. He asked Fremont to modify the proclamation, and later, when Fremont refused, ordered him to.

13. His wife, Jessie Benton Fremont. Lincoln did not change his mind, and Fremont changed the proclamation.

14. He was afraid it would cause Kentucky to leave the Union, and he was not convinced that it was legal to allow a military commander to free the slaves.

15. In Kentucky it was gratefully accepted, and acknowledged as an action that saved the state for the Union. In the loyal Northern states, it was severely criticized.

16. Nathaniel Gordon.

17. No.

18. To what two places did Lincoln consider colonizing slaves?

19. What happened to Lincoln's colonization plans?

20. In the summer of 1862, Lincoln proposed two plans to provide Federal funds to emancipate all of the slaves of what state?

21. What Union general, commanding Union forces occupying the coastal regions of South Carolina, Georgia, and Florida, proclaimed slaves in his military district "forever free" in May 1862?

22. What did Lincoln do about Hunter's proclamation?

23. What border state adopted a constitution outlawing slavery in October 1864?

24. What was the vote count in the first session of the 38th Congress when they attempted to pass the 13th Amendment, abolishing slavery?

25. How many Democrats voted in favor of the 13th Amendment, initially?

26. How many Democrats switched their vote on the 13th Amendment after Lincoln applied political pressure and used the patronage?

27. What did Lincoln call "a King's cures for all evils"?

18. To present-day Panama and an island near Haiti. Colonization to the African country of Liberia had already been in progress when Lincoln took office.

19. A small group of blacks were taken to an island near Haiti, but many died from disease, so the survivors were brought back to the United States. The Panama scheme was uncovered as the scam of opportunists, so it never took place.

20. Delaware. But the Delaware legislature was not supportive of the plans, and they were dropped.

21. General David Hunter, commander of the Department of the South.

22. He revoked it, as he had with Fremont's similar proclamation the preceding fall. However, in giving his reasons for revoking it, he made it obvious that although he still considered it inappropriate for a military commander to free the slaves, he believed it within his legal rights as president to free them.

23. Maryland.

24. The Senate passed it 38 to 6 on April 8, 1864, but the House of Representatives failed to attain the two thirds majority, 93 to 65.

25. Only four Democrats in the House voted in favor of it.

26. Thirteen. It passed by a vote of 119 to 56 on January 31, 1865.

27. The 13th Amendment. Lincoln was afraid that the Emancipation Proclamation would not be able to hold up against legal challenges after the war, and was glad when the permanent solution to the slavery issue was passed.

🏳 Lincoln and Kansas

1. What bill, passed by Congress on May 30, 1854, had the effect of rejuvenating the slavery debate in Congress and bringing Lincoln back into the political limelight?
2. What previous acts of Congress did the Kansas Nebraska Act supersede?
3. Who championed the Kansas Nebraska Act and successfully pushed it through Congress?
4. What were Lincoln's primary arguments against Kansas Nebraska?
5. What was the concept that people of the territories could allow or disallow slavery when the state was established called?
6. What was the Lecompton Constitution?
7. What were Lincoln's and Douglas's reactions to the Lecompton Constitution?
8. What was the impact, to the Democratic Party, of Douglas' opposition to the Lecompton Constitution?
9. How did Horace Greeley, editor of the powerful Republican newspaper the New York *Tribune*, react to Douglas' break with Buchanan over Lecompton?
10. What was the fate of the Lecompton Constitution?

✍ Lincoln and Kansas (Answers)

1. The Kansas Nebraska Act.
2. The Missouri Compromise of 1820 and the Compromise of 1850.
3. Stephen A. Douglas.
4. He believed that the nation's founders had intended slavery to eventually die out, and had consequently restricted slavery in the territories. But the Kansas Nebraska Act allowed slavery to go anywhere the local populace would accept it.
5. Popular Sovereignty.
6. Kansas' pro-slavery state constitution. It was supported by only a minority of the voters, but President Buchanan decided to accept it and push it through Congress anyway.
7. Both opposed it. Lincoln, because it was pro-slavery, and Douglas, because it was politically unpopular in Illinois and it did not comply with the spirit of his Popular Sovereignty doctrine.
8. There was a tremendous rift in the party, with Buchanan insisting on loyalty to himself, and Douglas refusing to give it.
9. He considered Douglas a hero and thought that the Illinois Republicans were foolish to oppose him in the Senate race.
10. It was defeated by Kansas voters on August 2, 1858, by a vote of 11,300 to 1,788.

Cooper Union Address

1. At what famous New York church was Lincoln invited to speak in February 1860?

2. Lincoln ordered a new suit especially for the lecture at Plymouth Church. Who made the suit for him, and how much did it cost?

3. By the time Lincoln arrived in New York for the address at the Plymouth Church, its sponsors and location had changed. What were the new sponsors and where was he to speak?

4. On what date was the Cooper Union Address?

5. Who was in the audience at Cooper Union?

6. How did the audience at Cooper Union react to Lincoln?

7. Why was Lincoln's Cooper Union engagement so important to Lincoln's political career?

8. Where did Lincoln go the day after the Cooper Union speech?

9. How long did Lincoln remain in New England after the Cooper Union speech?

10. On the same day as the Cooper Union Address, Lincoln had his photograph taken by what famous New York photographer?

✍ Cooper Union Address (Answers)

1. Henry Ward Beecher's Plymouth Church in Brooklyn.
2. Springfield tailors Woods and Henckle. $100.
3. The Young Men's Central Republican Union, in the Cooper Union in Manhattan.
4. February 27, 1860.
5. Various eastern intellectuals and abolitionists, including Henry Ward Beecher, William Cullen Bryant, and Horace Greeley.
6. Initially, they were appalled, because his voice was high and piercing, his suit wrinkled and ill-fitting, and his hair messed up. But during the course of his speech his voice became more melodious, they became fascinated with his excellent speech, and they gave him a standing ovation.
7. The audience was filled with politically influential people, many of whom went away with a favorable impression of Lincoln.
8. To visit his son Robert at the Phillips Exeter Academy in New England.
9. Two weeks. He traveled around Rhode Island, New Hampshire, Connecticut, and New York, making various speeches.
10. Matthew Brady.

Republican Presidential Nominee

1. What were the first newspapers to begin serious discussions about Lincoln for president?

2. Who were seven of the men that Lincoln entrusted with trying to work for his nomination to the Republican presidential ticket in 1860?

3. When and where did the Illinois State Republican Convention take place?

4. What was the catchy new political sobriquet given to Lincoln at Decatur?

5. Who was primarily responsible for giving Lincoln this sobriquet?

6. How did Oglesby sell the idea of Lincoln being called the Rail Candidate at the Illinois State Convention?

7. What did the sign, hung from the rails John Hanks carried, say?

8. What was Lincoln's strategy to secure the nomination at the 1860 Republican National Convention in Chicago?

9. What other city, besides Chicago, did the Republican National Committee consider for the 1860 convention?

10. Who, of Lincoln's circle of advisors, helped secure Chicago as the site of the convention?

11. Who were the four at-large delegates Lincoln chose to represent him at the Republican National Convention in Chicago?

12. What arrangement was made in regards to how the Illinois delegates would vote?

13. Why didn't Lincoln attend the Republican National Convention in Chicago?

14. Was Lincoln willing to accept the vice presidential slot on the ticket?

15. Who were the five primary candidates at the convention?

16. Why did Lincoln, a relative unknown, look so attractive as a presidential candidate for the Republicans?

✍ Republican Presidential Nominee (Answers)

1. The Lacon, Illinois, *Illinois Gazette*; the Sandusky, Ohio, *Sandusky Commercial Register*; and the Olney, Illinois, *Olney Times*. The latter began running "Abram Lincoln for President in 1860" below its masthead.

2. Judge David Davis, Norman Judd, Jesse Dubois, Ozias Hatch, Leonard Swett, Richard Yates, and Theodore Canisius.

3. May 9–10 in Decatur, Illinois.

4. The "Rail Candidate" or "Rail Splitter."

5. Richard J. Oglesby, a young politician from Decatur. He recognized that Lincoln needed a campaign slogan like President Harrison's "Log Cabin and Hard Cider."

6. He had Lincoln's elderly cousin John Hanks bring a couple of rails from a fence he and Lincoln had made 30 years ago to the convention, and march down the aisle with a sign.

7. "Abraham Lincoln the Rail Candidate—For President in 1860. Two rails made from a lot of 3,000 made in 1830 by Thos. Hanks and Abe Lincoln—whose father was the first pioneer of Macon County."

8. First, get the unanimous support of the Illinois delegates. Next, try to line up the second highest number of delegates behind Seward, and negotiate to get increasing number of votes on subsequent ballots.

9. St. Louis.

10. Norman Judd. Judd was a member of the Republican National Committee.

11. Norman Judd, Gustave P. Koerner, Orville H. Browning, and David Davis.

12. They would be unanimously for Lincoln.

13. In those days, it wasn't considered proper for the candidates themselves to go. So, Lincoln remained in Springfield and put Judge David Davis in charge.

14. No. He told men going to the convention that he would only accept the presidential nomination.

15. William H. Seward of New York (the favorite), Salmon P. Chase of Ohio, Edward Bates of Missouri, Simon Cameron of Pennsylvania, and Lincoln of Illinois.

16. He was solidly opposed to the expansion of slavery; he favored economic development and a protective tariff; he was popular with Whigs and had opposed the Know-Nothings without alienating them.

17. Why was the favorite, William H. Seward, vulnerable?

18. What did the Republicans call the assembly hall where they held the Republican National Convention?

19. How many people could the Wigwam seat, and how much did it cost to construct?

20. What directive did Lincoln telegram to David Davis regarding political bargains while they were at the convention?

21. Which candidate's representatives agreed to throw their votes to Lincoln on the second ballot if their man would be given a cabinet post by Lincoln?

22. How many votes were needed to win the nomination?

23. What were the first ballot tallies at the convention?

24. What were the second ballot tallies?

25. What were the third ballot tallies?

26. Who gave the winning votes to Lincoln?

27. Who were the two candidates considered for the vice presidential slot?

28. Who was selected as Lincoln's vice presidential running mate?

29. A few blocks from the Wigwam, on the second night of the convention, the McVickers Theatre opened with a theatrical play that would have future significance in Lincoln's life. What was the name of that play?

30. When and by whom was Lincoln officially notified that he had received the Republican nomination?

31. In the following weeks, when the number of guests and well-wishers became too numerous to be received in Lincoln's home, where did he begin meeting them?

32. Some of Lincoln's wealthy Springfield friends decided to hire a full time secretary for Lincoln. Whom did they hire, and for how much?

17. He had accumulated a lot of enemies in powerful places, such as New York *Tribune* editor Horace Greeley. He was also considered too "radical" on the slavery issue.

18. The "Wigwam."

19. About 10,000 people, and it cost about $6,000.

20. "Make no contracts that will bind me."

21. Those of Pennsylvania's Simon Cameron. Forty-four of Cameron's 46 and a half first ballot votes were switched to Lincoln on the second ballot. Historians have debated whether or not Davis actually pledged the cabinet position, but Lincoln evidently felt obligated to make Cameron secretary of war.

22. Two hundred thirty-three.

23. Seward, 173 and a half; Lincoln, 102; Cameron, 50 and a half; Chase, 49; Bates, 48. The other 42 votes were scattered among other miscellaneous candidates.

24. Seward, 184 and a half; Lincoln, 181; Chase, 42 and a half; Bates, 35; and Cameron, 2.

25. Seward, 180; Lincoln, 231 and a half; Chase, 24 and a half; Bates, 22.

26. D. K. Cartter of Ohio announced the switch of four Ohio votes from Salmon Chase to Lincoln immediately after the third ballot.

27. Cassius Clay of Kentucky and Hannibal Hamlin of Maine.

28. Hannibal Hamlin.

29. *Our American Cousin.* Lincoln would be watching this play the night he was assassinated nearly five years later.

30. On May 19, by a delegation headed by George Ashmun of Massachusetts, who came to Lincoln's home.

31. In the office of Governor John Wood in the State Capitol.

32. John Nicolay, a German-American newspaperman, for $75 per month.

1860 Presidential Campaign

1. When and where was the Democratic National Convention?
2. Over what issue did the Democratic Party split?
3. Who were the four political parties' candidates for the presidency in 1860?
4. Who were the "Wide Awakes"?
5. Did Lincoln vote for himself in the presidential election?
6. Did Lincoln make many speeches during the campaign?
7. Did Stephen A. Douglas follow the same policy as Lincoln as far as making speeches during the campaign?
8. In the election on November 6, how did the popular vote divide up among the candidates?
9. How did the electoral college vote split up?
10. What office did Lincoln tell a visitor a few days before he was elected president that he would rather have than presidency?
11. How many votes did Lincoln receive in the lower South?

✍ 1860 Presidential Campaign (Answers)

1. April 23, 1860, in Charleston, South Carolina.

2. Primarily whether or not slavery could be prohibited in the new territories—with Douglas insisting it could and Southern Democrats that it could not.

3. Stephen A. Douglas was the choice of the Northern Democrats; John C. Breckinridge of Kentucky was the choice of the Southern Democrats; John Bell of Tennessee was the Constitutional Union candidate; and Lincoln the Republican.

4. Young Republican men that marched in torchlight parades, singing and carrying rails in an effort to stir up support for the Republican Party.

5. No. He voted for local office seekers, but in following etiquette he did not vote for himself.

6. No. The candidates themselves were supposed to be above speech-making in those days.

7. No. Douglas broke with tradition and traveled all around the country, including the South, making speeches and urging reconciliation of North and South.

8. Lincoln, 1,866,452; Douglas, 1,376,957; Breckinridge, 849,781; and Bell, 588,879.

9. Lincoln, 180; Breckinridge, 72; Bell, 39; Douglas, 12.

10. United States senator.

11. None. In many places, his name wasn't even on the ballot.

🏳 Train Trip to Washington

1. When did Lincoln leave Springfield for Washington, D.C.?
2. What was the name of the locomotive that pulled the presidential train?
3. In his farewell speech to the people of Springfield, Lincoln said the task before him was greater than that faced by what other president?
4. How long did Lincoln's trip from Springfield to Washington take?
5. How many miles did the train travel?
6. Were Mary and the boys on the train when it left Springfield?
7. Who accompanied Lincoln on the train trip eastward, in addition to his family?
8. Through what major cities did the train travel?
9. Why did the train make such a long journey?
10. What did Lincoln typically say in his speeches to the crowds?
11. What special person did Lincoln ask to see when the presidential train stopped in Westfield, New York?
12. Who brought news to Lincoln of a possible plot to kill him when the presidential train passed through Baltimore?
13. Who did Pinkerton say planned to kill Lincoln in Baltimore?
14. What was Ferrandini's profession?
15. Where in Baltimore did they plan to kill Lincoln?
16. What did Pinkerton propose as a plan to keep this from happening?
17. Did Lincoln cancel his speech in Harrisburg?
18. Who brought word to Lincoln the next day that the threat Pinkerton spoke of was genuine?
19. How did Lincoln avoid the assassination attempt?

✍ Train Trip to Washington (Answers)

1. February 11, 1861. He departed via a special train that had been chartered for the purpose of taking him east.
2. The L. M. Wiley.
3. George Washington.
4. Twelve days.
5. One thousand nine hundred four miles.
6. No. They were in St. Louis on a shopping trip and had made arrangements to meet Lincoln in Indianapolis.
7. John Nicolay, John Hay, Dr. William S. Wallace, Elmer Ellsworth, Norman Judd, David Davis, Ozias Hatch, Jesse Dubois, Richard Yates, Colonel E. V. Summer, Major David Hunter, Captain John Pope, and Ward Hill Lamon.
8. Indianapolis, Cincinnati, Columbus, Pittsburgh, Cleveland, Buffalo, Albany, New York, Philadelphia, Harrisburg, and Baltimore.
9. In order to give the people the opportunity to see the president-elect. Large crowds gathered at the train depot of every city.
10. Very little of substance. He wanted to avoid making policy or political statements that would inflame the South, so he usually made small talk, ridiculed his own appearance, and complimented the ladies.
11. Grace Bedell, the 11-year-old girl that had written him, suggesting he grow a beard. She was brought up the platform to meet Lincoln.
12. Allan Pinkerton, of the Pinkerton National Protective Agency.
13. Cypriano Ferrandini and a handful of conspirators.
14. He was a barber in Baltimore.
15. Outside of the Calvert Street Railway Station, as he began his walk to the Camden Street Station across town.
16. That Lincoln cancel his address to the Pennsylvania legislature in Harrisburg the next day, and pass through Baltimore on a train that evening.
17. No. He said he was going to go through with his commitments, "even if he met death in doing so."
18. Frederick W. Seward, son of Senator Seward who, along with General Winfield Scott, had substantiated what Pinkerton said.
19. He, Pinkerton, and Ward Lamon left on a special train the evening before he was scheduled to go to Baltimore and went through Baltimore in the middle of the night, arriving in Washington early in the morning.

20. How was Lincoln disguised during the trip in order to avoid recognition?
21. Who met Lincoln at the train station in Washington?
22. How did the press react to Lincoln's night trip through Baltimore?

20. He wore a soft felt "Kossuth" hat and wore a long overcoat, thrown over his shoulders.
21. Congressman E. B. Washburn, an old friend from Illinois.
22. They ridiculed it, with cartoons showing Lincoln sneaking into Washington in a scotch cap and kilts.

⚑ Fort Sumter

1. As the Southern states declared their independence, they took over all but two Federal forts and arsenals within their borders. What two did they not take over?

2. What ship did President James Buchanan send to Charleston Harbor in an attempt to provision Fort Sumter with supplies and troops?

3. The morning after the inauguration, Lincoln received a report from what officer that indicated he would have to surrender Fort Sumter within six weeks if it was not resupplied?

4. How large of a military force did Major Anderson estimate it would take to properly reinforce his fort?

5. How many men did Major Anderson have defending Fort Sumter?

6. On March 15, 1861, Lincoln asked each member of his cabinet to respond to the question of whether or not he should attempt to provision Fort Sumter. How did each cabinet member vote?

7. Lincoln sent what three men to Charleston to assess the situation there?

8. What did Horace Greeley of the New York *Tribune* recommend Lincoln do about Fort Sumter?

9. What senior military officer advised Lincoln on March 28 to abandon both Fort Sumter in Charleston Harbor and Fort Pickens in Pensacola, Florida?

10. Why was Seward so adamant about evacuating Fort Sumter?

11. On April 6, whom did Lincoln send to Charleston to warn South Carolina Governor Francis Pickens that he was sending nonmilitary provisions to Fort Sumter via ship?

12. What did President Davis decide to do when he heard the fort would be resupplied?

13. At what date and time was the first shot fired at Fort Sumter?

14. How long did the Confederate bombardment last before Fort Sumter surrendered?

15. How many casualties had Major Anderson's men sustained when defending the fort?

🖋 Fort Sumter (Answers)

1. Fort Sumter in Charleston Harbor and Fort Pickens at Pensacola, Florida.

2. The *Star of the West*. Southern forts fired on her on January 9, 1861, preventing her entrance to the harbor.

3. Major Robert Anderson, commander of Fort Sumter in Charleston Harbor.

4. Twenty-five thousand.

5. Anderson had a total of 128 men, many of whom were workmen and musicians.

6. Seward, Cameron, Welles, and Smith said no and thought the fort should be surrendered. Chase and Blair thought it should be provisioned and held.

7. Gustavus Fox, a former navy lieutenant; Stephen A. Hurlbut, an old Illinois friend, and Ward H. Lamon, his friend and associate from the Eighth Judicial Circuit.

8. He was opposed to Lincoln's use of force to keep the fort and suggested that Lincoln let the South secede without opposition.

9. General Winfield Scott, commander of the army. In saying this, he was repeating the sentiments of William H. Seward.

10. He had been holding secret communications with Southern leaders, assuring them that Lincoln would abandon the fort.

11. Robert S. Chew, a clerk in the State Department.

12. Attack it.

13. The Confederate bombardment started on April 12, 1861, at 4:30 A.M.

14. Thirty-three hours.

15. None. A man was killed, however, when a cannon exploded during the surrender ceremonies.

🏳 War Begins

1. When did Lincoln issue his proclamation calling for the states to provide militia to put down the rebellion?
2. How many troops did Lincoln call for?
3. Why did Lincoln ask for the militia to serve for only 90 days?
4. How did the governors of the still-loyal states react to Lincoln's call for volunteers to put down the rebellion?
5. Why did Lincoln insist on calling it a "rebellion"?
6. On April 18, what Union regiment was attacked by a Baltimore mob as it passed through the city?
7. What request did Governor Hicks of Maryland make of Lincoln regarding the reinforcements that were coming to Washington?
8. What Union general that had previously been an influential member of Congress took a military force and occupied Federal Hill in Baltimore, intimidating secessionists?
9. When did Lincoln first authorize suspension of habeas corpus, and where?
10. Who was the Maryland resident that was arrested, held in Fort McHenry without trial, and then attempted to secure his freedom by obtaining a writ of habeas corpus from Chief Justice Taney?
11. What did Lincoln do when Chief Justice Taney ordered him to release Merryman?
12. Did Congress support Lincoln's suspension of the writ?
13. What two Baltimore officials were arrested and held without bail?
14. On September 17, 1861, how many members of the Maryland legislature were arrested and why?
15. Whom did Lincoln appoint as commander of the Department of Kentucky?
16. When did the states of Tennessee, Arkansas, Virginia, and North Carolina secede?

✍ War Begins (Answers)

1. April 15, 1861—the day after Fort Sumter surrendered.

2. Seventy-five thousand men for 90 days of service.

3. Because a 1795 law limited a call-up of militia to not more than 30 days after assembling Congress—which Lincoln had designated to occur on July 4.

4. Eight governors refused (Arkansas, Tennessee, North Carolina, Virginia, Kentucky, Missouri, Maryland, and Delaware), but the others enthusiastically agreed to do so. Delaware's governor allowed volunteer regiments to offer their services independently.

5. He took the position that secession was illegal, that the South never legally left the Union, and that there was not really a separate nation called "the Confederate States of America." In future speeches, when he had to refer to the South, he would usually call it "the so-called Confederate States of America."

6. The 6th Massachusetts Regiment. Four soldiers and 12 civilians were killed.

7. First, that they not be marched through Baltimore, to which Lincoln concurred. Later, he asked that they not march through Maryland at all, which Lincoln refused.

8. Benjamin F. Butler.

9. On April 27, 1861, along the route between Philadelphia and Washington. This gave Lincoln the authority to have anyone aiding the Confederate cause or disrupting the arrival of Union troops arrested and held in jail without trial.

10. John Merryman, a lieutenant of a secessionist drill company in Cockeysville, Maryland.

11. He ignored him.

12. Yes. They eventually passed the Habeas Corpus Indemnity Act, affirming Lincoln's right to suspend the writ but requiring the secretaries of state and war to provide a list of incarcerated persons.

13. George P. Kane, Baltimore's police marshal, and Mayor William Brown.

14. Nine members of the legislature and the chief clerk of the Maryland Senate were arrested because the local military authority suspected they were going to try to take Maryland out of the Union.

15. Robert Anderson, hero of Fort Sumter.

16. After Lincoln's call for 75,000 volunteers to put down the rebellion. Virginia seceded April 17, 1861; Arkansas on May 6; North Carolina on May 21; and Tennessee on June 8.

17. How did the people of the westernmost counties of Virginia react to their state's secession?

18. How did the people of the westernmost counties of Virginia apply for statehood?

19. Who was the governor elected by the Wheeling convention?

20. On May 3, Lincoln called for how many additional volunteer soldiers?

21. On what day did Lincoln proclaim a naval blockade of Southern ports?

22. After the Southern states' representatives left Congress, what percentage of the Senate and House of Representatives were Republican?

23. How much money did Lincoln ask of Congress to prosecute the war when they reconvened on July 4, and how much did Congress authorize?

24. How many men did Lincoln ask Congress to authorize for the army, and how many did they authorize?

25. What personal friend of Lincoln's was killed by an Alexandria, Virginia, hotelkeeper on May 24?

26. When did the US Congress officially recognize a state of war existed?

17. They decided to secede, in turn, from Virginia.

18. They sent representatives to Wheeling to set up a rival government to the Confederate Virginia government and elected their own governor. This governor approved the separation of the western counties, which applied for statehood and eventually became West Virginia.

19. Francis H. Pierpont.

20. Forty-two thousand thirty-four. He also increased the size of the regular army to 22,714 and asked for 18,000 additional seamen.

21. April 19, 1861.

22. Sixty-six percent of the Senate and 60 percent of the House.

23. $400,000,000. Congress authorized $500,000,000.

24. Lincoln requested 400,000 and Congress authorized 500,000.

25. Elmer Ellsworth. He had led a regiment of Zouave troops into the town and was shot by the hotelkeeper after tearing down a secessionist flag at the top of the building.

26. July 13, 1861.

♫ Battles

1. When and where was the first significant battle in Virginia?

2. How many men were engaged at the battle of First Manassas and who won the battle?

3. What long-time friend of Lincoln's was killed in the Battle of Ball's Bluff on October 21, 1861?

4. What obscure Union brigadier general captured Confederate Fort Henry on the Tennessee River on February 6, 1862?

5. What other Confederate fort did he capture, 11 days later?

6. What battle in western Tennessee on April 6-7, 1862, became the bloodiest fought on the American continent up to that time?

7. After Shiloh, why did Grant's superior, General Halleck, try to remove Grant from command?

8. What did Lincoln say when Grant's removal was proposed by the War Department?

9. What was the Seven Days Campaign?

10. What was the result of the Battle of Second Manassas (Bull Run) on August 28-30?

11. What did Lee decide to do after defeating Pope?

12. What military victory by McClellan had the double benefit of turning back Lee's invasion and giving Lincoln his excuse to issue the Emancipation Proclamation?

13. Who won the Battle of Fredericksburg, on December 13, 1862?

14. What was the result of the Battle of Stones River in central Tennessee on January 2, 1863, and who were the opposing commanders?

15. On April 28, 1863, General Joseph Hooker began moving troops across the Rappahannock River to begin the Battle of Chancellorsville. What were the results of this battle?

✍ Battles (Answers)

1. On July 21, at Manassas, Virginia (known as the First Battle of Bull Run by Northerners).
2. About 60,000 total. Confederate victory.
3. Edward D. Baker, after whom Lincoln had named his second son. Baker was a colonel of volunteers.
4. Ulysses S. Grant.
5. Fort Donelson.
6. The Battle of Shiloh, also called Pittsburg's Landing. They were nearly 24,000 in killed, wounded, and missing.
7. Grant had been surprised by the Confederate army under Albert S. Johnston at Shiloh and was nearly defeated. Halleck said that Grant had been drinking, but really was just fabricating an excuse to remove a subordinate commander that was starting to overshadow him.
8. "I can't spare this man, he fights." Grant was not dismissed, but was temporarily placed second in command of his army because of Halleck's arrival to take command.
9. A series of engagements in the spring of 1862 in which Lee attacked McClellan and pushed him back from the gates of Richmond to Harrison's Landing on the James River.
10. Robert E. Lee and his Army of Northern Virginia, which had slipped away from McClellan on the peninsula, defeated General John Pope and his Army of Virginia.
11. Invade the North.
12. The Battle of Antietam (also called Sharpsburg) on September 17, 1862. This was the bloodiest single day in American history, with approximately 23,000 Americans killed, wounded, or missing.
13. The Confederates, under Robert E. Lee, defeated the Union army under Ambrose Burnside. It was, up to that time, the worst defeat for Union armies.
14. A marginal Union victory. The Union army was commanded by General William S. Rosecrans, the Southern army by General Braxton Bragg.
15. Hooker was defeated by Lee and retreated back across the Rappahannock on May 6. Stonewall Jackson died.

16. What did Hooker propose to Lincoln he should do with the Army of the Potomac if Lee invaded the North?

17. What was the result of the three-day battle of Gettysburg?

18. What other major victory for Union arms took place on July 4?

19. What were the results of the Battle of Chickamauga on September 19 and 20, 1863?

20. What was the result of Grant's first battle with Lee at the Wilderness in the spring of 1864?

21. What Southern city, when captured by Union General William T. Sherman in September 1864, virtually assured Lincoln's victory in the presidential election and ultimate Union victory?

22. Grant pushed Lee back during the summer of 1864 until he began a siege at what city south of Richmond?

23. What Confederate commander made an unsuccessful raid on Washington, D.C., in July 1864?

24. How many men did Early have with him?

25. How close did Early get to Washington, D.C.?

26. Did Lincoln witness the Confederate attack?

27. What did Captain Oliver Wendell Holmes, Jr. purportedly shout at Lincoln when he saw him standing on the parapet of Fort Stevens, watching the fighting?

28. Who else of the Lincoln family accompanied the president to Fort Stevens on the second day of the Confederate attack?

29. What decisive battle in Tennessee all but annihilated the western Confederate army under the command of John Bell Hood on December 15 and 16, 1864?

16. Move south and take Richmond. Lincoln told him, however, that Lee's army was his objective, not Richmond.

17. Lee was defeated by Meade and began his retreat the next day, on July 4, 1863. There were approximately 50,000 casualties between the two armies.

18. Confederate General John C. Pemberton surrendered the city of Vicksburg, Mississippi, and his army of 30,000 men to U. S. Grant.

19. The Union army, under William S. Rosecrans, was defeated by General Braxton Bragg. Rosecrans retreated to Chattanooga, Tennessee, which was quickly put under siege by the Confederate army.

20. Although Grant was repulsed by Lee, he continued to march southward toward Richmond.

21. Atlanta.

22. Petersburg, Virginia.

23. Jubal A. Early, with the Second Corps of the Army of Northern Virginia.

24. Fifteen thousand.

25. He advanced down from the north, through Silver Spring, and got all the way to Fort Stevens on the outskirts of Washington before being driven back.

26. Yes. He went to Fort Stevens during both days of the Confederates' attack.

27. "Get down, you damn fool, before you get shot!" It was reported that Holmes shouted this before he recognized who Lincoln was, but there is debate among historians today as to whether or not Holmes really said anything to Lincoln.

28. Mary.

29. The Battle of Nashville, won by Union commander George H. Thomas.

⌂ Lincoln's Cabinet

1. Who was on Lincoln's initial list of potential presidential cabinet members?

2. When and where, after the election, did Lincoln meet with his future vice president, Hannibal Hamlin?

3. Whom did Lincoln send to William H. Seward with the news that he wanted him to be his secretary of state?

4. What North Carolina Whig did Lincoln consider appointing to a cabinet post?

5. Whom, from the South, did Lincoln choose instead of Gilmer?

6. Who became Lincoln's secretary of the treasury?

7. Who became Lincoln's attorney general?

8. Who became Lincoln's secretary of the interior?

9. To whom did Lincoln offer a cabinet position, withdraw it, and then offer it again?

10. Why did Lincoln withdraw the offer to Cameron?

11. Who became Lincoln's secretary of the navy?

12. Who were the only men to remain in Lincoln's cabinet throughout his entire presidency?

13. Why was Cameron called, derisively, the "Great Winnebago Chief"?

14. Whom did Lincoln name as minister to England?

15. What two cabinet positions did Lincoln finally offer to Cameron?

16. On March 2, why did Lincoln's proposed secretary of state, William H. Seward, request to be allowed to withdraw from his cabinet position?

17. What did Lincoln say about Seward's proposed withdrawal from the cabinet?

18. What two extraordinary things did Seward suggest in his April 1 letter entitled "some thoughts for the president's consideration"?

✍ Lincoln's Cabinet (Answers)

1. William H. Seward, Edward Bates, William C. Dayton, Norman Judd, Salmon P. Chase, Montgomery Blair, and Gideon Welles.

2. November 21-23, 1861, in Chicago. He had never met Hamlin face to face before.

3. Hannibal Hamlin. Lincoln was concerned that Seward might still be sensitive of his defeat at the Republican National Convention, and wanted to entrust this task to a politician experienced in Washington politics.

4. John A. Gilmer. But Lincoln turned him down when Gilmer insisted on Federal protection of slavery in the territories as a precondition of his acceptance.

5. Montgomery Blair of Maryland.

6. Salmon P. Chase of Ohio.

7. Edward Bates of Missouri.

8. Caleb B. Smith of Indiana.

9. Simon Cameron of Pennsylvania. Cameron was considered for both the War and Treasury Departments.

10. A. K. McClure convinced Lincoln, after the initial offer, that Cameron was morally unfit for office. But a lack of hard evidence against Cameron and political pressures caused Lincoln to change his mind.

11. Gideon Welles of Connecticut. Lincoln allowed Hamlin to pick someone from New England for the cabinet, and Hamlin chose Welles.

12. Seward and Welles.

13. When previously appointed by President Van Buren to be commissioner to settle claims of the Winnebago Indians, he had purportedly defrauded them of $66,000.

14. Charles Francis Adams of New England.

15. War and Interior. Cameron chose War, but really wanted the Treasury.

16. He was offended that Lincoln had selected one of his political rivals, Salmon Chase, for the Secretary of the Treasury.

17. He said he couldn't "afford to let Seward take the first trick," and convinced Seward to stay.

18. First, that Lincoln find an excuse to declare war on France and Spain, hoping it would bring the South to the North's aid and back into the Union. Second, that he, Seward, should take charge of administering the government.

19. When and why did Lincoln replace Simon Cameron as secretary of war?

20. Who secretly authored Cameron's report to Congress that endorsed freeing slaves?

21. With whom did Lincoln replace Cameron at the War Department?

22. To what political party did Stanton belong?

23. What were two of Stanton's greatest personal attributes that attracted Lincoln to him?

24. Which cabinet member drafted a protest of Lincoln's action putting McClellan in command of the combined force of the Army of the Potomac and the Army of Virginia after Pope's defeat at Second Manassas?

25. How often did Lincoln have cabinet meetings?

26. Which member of Lincoln's cabinet surprised the president with his resignation on December 16, 1862?

27. Which member of Lincoln's cabinet had been influential in getting the Senate to consider the "no confidence" vote in Seward?

28. What was Chase's primary complaint about Lincoln?

29. How did Lincoln defeat the senators' attempt to force the resignation of Seward?

30. What action did Chase take after this cabinet meeting?

31. Whose image was on the first one dollar bill?

32. Which member of Lincoln's cabinet made a serious effort to unseat Lincoln as the Republican Party's nominee for president in 1864?

33. What political circular distributed by Chase's followers in February 1864 proposed that Chase, not Lincoln, was the best choice for Republican nominee for president?

34. What did Chase offer Lincoln as a result of the "Pomeroy Circular"?

35. When did Chase withdraw from the presidential contest?

36. What cabinet officer offered to resign in June 1864?

19. January 11, 1862. Cameron had proven incompetent in the War Department, and when he prepared a report for Congress endorsing the idea of freeing and arming slaves, without Lincoln's approval, Lincoln replaced him. Lincoln offered him the post of minister to Russia.

20. Edwin Stanton.

21. Edwin Stanton. Stanton was the lawyer that had insulted Lincoln on the McCormick Reaper case seven years earlier.

22. Democratic. He was a War Democrat.

23. Intelligence and honesty.

24. Stanton. He managed to get Chase, Smith, and Bates to sign it, but Welles refused and it is likely that neither Seward nor Blair saw it.

25. Normally, twice a week. Tuesdays and Thursdays, in the afternoon.

26. Secretary of State William H. Seward. The reason he offered his resignation was that the Senate was seriously considering a resolution declaring a lack of confidence in the secretary of state.

27. Secretary of the Treasury Salmon P. Chase. Chase and Seward had always been rivals, and Chase complained about Seward and Lincoln to friends in the Senate.

28. That he didn't consult with his cabinet properly and seek concurrence in decisions before making them.

29. Lincoln called several senators to a cabinet meeting and asked his cabinet if they concurred that they were usually consulted on decisions, and the results were harmonious. Chase did not have the nerve to repeat his charges in front of Lincoln.

30. He offered his resignation to Lincoln. Lincoln was consequently able to refuse the resignations of both Chase and Seward and keep his cabinet intact. The Senate dropped the lack of confidence vote.

31. Salmon P. Chase's.

32. Secretary of the Treasury Salmon P. Chase.

33. The "Pomeroy Circular," named after Senator Samuel C. Pomeroy, who signed it. It had an adverse backlash on Chase, even though he claimed to not have seen it before it was distributed and published in the newspapers.

34. His resignation. Lincoln refused it.

35. Officially, March 5. But he always kept his options open.

36. Secretary of the Treasury Salmon P. Chase. This time Lincoln accepted Chase's resignation.

37. Whom did Lincoln first nominate to be Chase's replacement?

38. Who became Chase's replacement as secretary of the treasury?

39. What member of Lincoln's cabinet was approached by moderate Republicans and asked to lead a "centrist" party ticket in the 1864 presidential elections?

40. What memorandum did Lincoln ask his entire cabinet to sign in August 1864, without allowing them to read it first?

41. What cabinet member did Lincoln agree to ask to resign if radical congressmen Ben Wade and Henry Winter Davis would support his re-election and John C. Fremont would drop out of the race for the Republican nomination?

42. Did Blair resign when Fremont dropped out of the race?

43. With whom did Lincoln replace Blair as postmaster general?

44. With whom did Lincoln replace Attorney General Bates in his cabinet?

45. With whom did Lincoln replace Secretary of the Interior Usher?

46. With whom, in the winter of 1864–1865, did Lincoln replace Secretary of the Treasury Fessenden?

47. Who were some of the candidates Lincoln considered for appointment to Supreme Court Justice when Chief Justice Roger Taney died on October 12, 1864?

48. Whom did Lincoln finally appoint as chief justice?

37. David Tod, former governor of Ohio. He declined Lincoln's nomination due to bad health.

38. Senator William P. Fessenden of Maine.

39. William H. Seward. But Seward refused, and said that he thought Lincoln "the best and wisest man (he) has ever known."

40. Since it appeared to Lincoln that he may not win the presidential election in November, he wrote out a memorandum acknowledging this fact and insisting it would be the duty of his administration to work with the new president-elect in order to save the Union before the latter took office.

41. Montgomery Blair, postmaster general. Blair had become a political liability, but Lincoln was still reluctant to ask him to resign.

42. Yes.

43. Governor William Dennison of Ohio.

44. James Speed of Kentucky, brother of Lincoln's old friend Joshua Speed.

45. Senator James Harlan of Iowa.

46. Hugh McCulloch, comptroller of the currency.

47. Salmon P. Chase, Edwin Stanton, Edmond Bates, and Montgomery Blair.

48. Salmon P. Chase.

🏳 Lincoln and the Military

1. How many men were in the US Army when Lincoln took office as president?

2. When did General Winfield Scott retire?

3. When were the Union troops around Washington first given the name "Army of the Potomac"?

4. In the summer of 1861, whom did General Scott put in field command of the Union army that was to advance from Washington to Richmond?

5. Once, when Lincoln was reviewing the troops, a soldier complained to him that his colonel, William T. Sherman, had threatened to shoot him if he left for New York without leave. What did Lincoln say in response?

6. What book on military strategy did Lincoln borrow from the Library of Congress in early 1862?

7. In the spring of 1862, Lincoln recalled what old soldier from retirement to act as his military advisor?

8. What famous naval battle took place at Hampton Roads, Virginia, on March 9, 1862?

9. Which ship won this battle?

10. Had Lincoln supported the development of the ironclad *Monitor*?

11. On July 11, 1862, Lincoln named what western general as commander in chief of all Union armies?

12. Lincoln assembled a new eastern army after McClellan and the Army of the Potomac had been defeated in the Seven Days campaign. What was the name of the new army and who was its commander?

13. What happened to Pope after he lost the Battle of Second Manassas?

14. In central Tennessee, Lincoln replaced General Carlos Buell, who commanded the Army of the Ohio, with what new commander in October of 1862?

15. Why did Lincoln replace Buell?

16. In August 1862 a Sioux Indian uprising in Minnesota killed how many white settlers?

✍ Lincoln and the Military (Answers)

1. About 16,000—most of which were in outposts along the Indian frontier.
2. November 1, 1861.
3. After August 15, 1861.
4. General Irvin McDowell. He was a 42-year-old graduate of West Point that had served in the Mexican War.
5. "Well, if I were you, and he threatened to shoot, I would not trust him, for I believe he would do it." Lincoln said it loud enough for others to hear.
6. Henry W. Halleck's *Elements of Military Art and Science.*
7. Sixty-four-year-old Ethan Allen Hitchcock, grandson of the Revolutionary War hero. Although he continued to serve throughout the war, Hitchcock provided little in the way of useful military advice.
8. The USS *Monitor* and the CSS *Virginia*, formerly the USS *Merrimac.*
9. Basically, it was a draw. Neither ship was able to do serious damage to the other.
10. Yes. When Lincoln met with a navy board, whose members were skeptical of the value of the new ship, he indicated his support of the *Monitor* by saying, "All I have to say is what the girl said when she put her foot into the stocking. It strikes me there's something in it."
11. Henry W. Halleck, Grant's immediate superior.
12. The Army of Virginia, commanded by General John Pope. Pope had been one of the officers that had accompanied Lincoln on his train trip from Springfield to Washington.
13. He was relieved of command. His army was put under the authority of McClellan and sent northward to fight Lee.
14. William S. Rosecrans.
15. He had repeatedly refused to go to the aid of the pro-Union population of eastern Tennessee, who were being persecuted by Confederate authorities.
16. Over 350. It was the largest massacre of whites by Indians in American history.

17. Why had the Sioux uprising occurred?

18. Whom did Lincoln send west to put down the uprising?

19. What message did Lincoln send to Pope when he found out the general had crushed the uprising and was preparing to put over 1,500 Indians on trial?

20. Whom did Lincoln send to investigate the uprising?

21. How many Sioux Indians did the military courts recommend hanging?

22. Lincoln personally reviewed each case and decreased the number of hangings to how many?

23. What did Lincoln say to Senator Ramsey of Minnesota, who later told Lincoln that if he had hung more Indians, the Republican Party would have remained more popular in that state?

24. In December 1862, General Grant embarrassed the Lincoln administration by banning what class of settlers and traders from his army?

25. What military operation did Lincoln personally direct while McClellan was engaged in his movement up the peninsula towards Richmond?

26. What happened to the Confederate ironclad *Virginia (Merrimac)* as a result of Lincoln's order to take Norfolk?

27. With whom did Lincoln replace McClellan as commander of the Army of the Potomac in November 1862?

28. With whom did Lincoln replace Burnside as commander of the Army of the Potomac in early 1863?

29. Prior to being appointed commander, Hooker had told a reporter that the country needed a new type of leader. What did Hooker say that leader should be?

30. How many military pardons did Lincoln grant?

31. Why did Hooker resign his position as commander of the Army of the Potomac a few days before the Battle of Gettysburg?

32. With whom did Lincoln replace Hooker?

33. On July 13, draft riots began in what Northern city?

34. How many people died in these riots?

17. Because bureaucratic delays had prevented the timely payment of annuities the Indians were supposed to receive for their land, and many were beginning to starve.

18. General John Pope, recently removed from command of the Army of Virginia.

19. He told him to stage no executions without permission from the White House.

20. Assistant Secretary of the Interior John P. Usher.

21. Three hundred three. Some of them had been convicted of murder and rape.

22. Thirty-nine. Thirty-eight were actually hung, in the largest public execution in American history.

23. "I could not afford to hang men for votes."

24. Jews. Lincoln revoked this order.

25. The capture of Norfolk, Virginia. Lincoln personally scouted out a landing place for the troops the night before he ordered their landing and attack of Norfolk.

26. The Confederates blew it up in order to prevent capture.

27. Ambrose E. Burnside.

28. General Joseph Hooker, commander of the Center Grand Division of the Army of the Potomac.

29. A dictator. Lincoln wrote to Hooker, when he placed him in command, the following comment about the dictator quip: "it was not for this, but in spite of it, that I have given you command . . . what I now ask of you is military success, and I will risk the dictatorship."

30. At least 225.

31. He had been ordered by General Halleck to maintain a strong garrison at Harper's Ferry, but Hooker wanted to concentrate all his forces to the north where Lee's main army was. He probably thought that his resignation would be rejected, but it was not.

32. General George Gordon Meade, commander of the V Corps of the Army of the Potomac. He put Meade in command on June 28, just three days before the battle of Gettysburg.

33. New York.

34. Over a hundred.

35. How were the riots finally stopped?

36. What did General Sherman offer Lincoln as a "Christmas gift" in 1864?

37. To what rank was Grant promoted on March 9, 1864?

38. How was the military strategy employed by Grant different than that of his predecessors, and what did Lincoln think of it?

39. Where did Lincoln, Mary, and Tad go on March 23, 1865, in order to visit Union troops and get away from Washington for a few days?

40. What was the name of the boat they sailed on?

41. Who else accompanied the Lincolns from Washington?

42. While at City Point, Mary became angry at the wife of which Union general when she accompanied Lincoln on a review of the troops?

43. How long did Lincoln and Tad stay at City Point?

44. Which three military commanders did Lincoln have a conference with aboard the *River Queen* on March 28, 1864?

45. At the conference with Grant, Sherman, and Porter, how did Lincoln say he wanted the Confederate soldiers treated once they were ready to surrender?

46. When did Lincoln return to Washington from City Point?

47. When did Lincoln learn of Lee's surrender?

48. How many cannon were fired around Washington on April 10 in celebration of Lee's surrender?

35. By troops brought up from Gettysburg.

36. The City of Savannah, Georgia, which he had captured after his march through Georgia.

37. Lieutenant general and commander in chief of all Union armies. He was only the second American to ever hold that high rank. General Washington was the first. General Scott had held the rank of brevet lieutenant general, only.

38. Grant proposed to have all the North's major armies advance simultaneously against the Confederate forces that opposed them. Lincoln was delighted with this strategy, as he had been encouraging simultaneous advances for years.

39. To City Point, Virginia, to visit Grant and the Army of the Potomac.

40. The *River Queen.*

41. Mary Lincoln's maid, Captain Charles Penrose, and White House guard William H. Crook.

42. General O. O. Ord's wife, Mary. Mary called Mrs. Ord insulting names and deeply embarrassed Lincoln.

43. Over two weeks. Mary went back to Washington earlier.

44. General U. S. Grant, General William T. Sherman, and Admiral David D. Porter.

45. He wanted generous terms of surrender offered and wanted them treated magnanimously.

46. Late in the afternoon of April 9.

47. The evening of April 9. Lee had surrendered to Grant earlier in the day, accepting magnanimous terms that allowed the soldiers to go back to their homes and take any horse or mule with them they claimed to be their own.

48. Five hundred.

꘎ McClellan

1. After the battle of First Manassas, what previously victorious Union general did Lincoln bring from western Virginia to take over field command around Washington?
2. What did Lincoln call "General McClellan's bodyguard"?
3. What were some of the insulting nicknames McClellan called Lincoln?
4. How did McClellan insult Lincoln, Seward, and John Hay one night when he came home late and found the three men waiting to talk to him in his parlor?
5. What approach to Richmond did McClellan propose to take in the spring of 1862?
6. Which army corps did Lincoln elect to hold back for the defense of Washington after McClellan and the Army of the Potomac had begun their departure for the James River peninsula?
7. What Confederate military operation caused Lincoln to divert a large part of McDowell's force from reinforcing McClellan on the peninsula?
8. What officer from Halleck's staff did Lincoln dismiss from the army because he had publicly stated it was not McClellan's intention to openly defeat the Confederate armies?
9. On what date did Lincoln go out to visit McClellan and visit the Antietam battlefield?
10. While traversing the Antietam Battlefield in an ambulance, what sad song did Lincoln ask his friend Ward Lamon to sing?
11. Why did Lincoln regret asking Lamon to sing that song?
12. How many days after Antietam was it before McClellan finally advanced the Army of the Potomac into Virginia to pursue Lee?
13. What did Lincoln telegraph McClellan when the latter complained, on October 24, 1862, that his cavalry could not pursue Lee because his horses were fatigued?
14. When and why did Lincoln remove McClellan from command?
15. With whom did Lincoln replace McClellan?

✍ McClellan (Answers)

1. General George B. McClellan.
2. The Army of the Potomac.
3. Well-meaning Baboon, Rare Bird, Old Stick, and Gorilla.
4. He went to bed without speaking to them.
5. McClellan proposed moving the Army of the Potomac via transports to the peninsula between the York and James Rivers, and advance on Richmond from the east.
6. McDowell's Corps. Lincoln was afraid that McClellan had left insufficient military force to protect Washington.
7. Stonewall Jackson's military diversion in the Shenandoah Valley in the spring of 1862. Lincoln became involved in trying to capture Jackson's force and ordered McDowell to reinforce Union troops in the Shenandoah Valley.
8. Major John J. Key. Key's brother was a member of McClellan's staff, and Lincoln probably intended the cashiering of Key to be a message to McClellan and his officers that the war must be prosecuted vigorously.
9. October 1, 1862.
10. "Twenty Years Ago."
11. The newspapers heard of the incident, and blew the story out of proportion, claiming that Lincoln and Lamon insulted the dead and wounded by singing ribald songs and playing a banjo while traversing the battlefield.
12. Nineteen.
13. "Will you pardon me for asking what the horses of your army have done since the battle of Antietam that fatigue anything?"
14. On November 5, 1862, the day after the last of the fall elections. He decided McClellan wasn't going to attack Lee before winter, as he had requested him to do.
15. General Ambrose P. Burnside, who had commanded the IX Corps at Antietam.

⚑ Congress and Lincoln

1. What Congressional Committee was formed as a result of the Ball's Bluff disaster?
2. Who were the members of the Committee on the Conduct of the War?
3. What were some of the most notable accomplishments of the 37th Congress?
4. Did Lincoln usually present his messages to Congress in person?
5. Whom did Lincoln try to promote as Speaker of the House for the 38th Congress?
6. Who was Lincoln's second choice for Speaker of the House?
7. Who became Speaker of the House for the 38th Congress?
8. What radical Republican senator became close friends with both Lincoln and Mary in 1864?
9. What was the Wade-Davis bill?
10. What action did Lincoln take on the Wade-Davis bill?

✍ Congress and Lincoln (Answers)

1. The Joint Committee on the Conduct of the War, which became a standing committee with representatives from both the House and Senate responsible for investigating various issues, primarily military, during the course of the war.

2. Senator Benjamin F. Wade, chairman; Andrew Johnson, Zachariah Chandler, George Washington Julian, John Covode, Daniel Gooch, Moses Odell, Joseph A. Wright, Benjamin F. Harding, and Charles R. Buckalew.

3. The National Banking Act, the Homestead Act, the transcontinental railroad, the establishment of a system of land grant colleges, the establishment of the Department of Agriculture, and the establishment of an internal revenue law that permanently altered the nation's tax structure.

4. No. They were usually read by a clerk.

5. Major General Frank Blair, the brother of Postmaster General Montgomery Blair. Frank Blair was a corps commander in Sherman's army, but did not arrive in Washington in time for the organization of Congress.

6. E. B. Washburn, his old friend from Illinois. Washburn was never seriously considered by the Republican leadership, however, and did not attain the position.

7. Schuyler Colfax of Indiana.

8. Senator Charles Sumner.

9. A bill that required any Southern state attempting to regain full recognition to first accept full abolition of slavery, and that 50 percent of its voters must participate in elections to reinstate the government, but those 50 percent must swear that they had never borne arms against the US or aided the rebellion.

10. Believing it too harsh, Lincoln used the pocket veto on the bill, something that had rarely been used before.

♆ Emancipation

1. Lincoln signed Congress's First Confiscation Act on August 6, 1861. What did that act do?

2. On what date did Lincoln formally propose to Congress that it provide funds to states for the purchase and emancipation of slaves?

3. What happened as a result of Lincoln's March 6 proposal?

4. When was the bill authorizing compensated emancipation of slaves in the District of Columbia signed by Lincoln?

5. When did Lincoln change his mind about adding emancipation of the slaves to the war aims?

6. What was the name of the book that was instrumental in convincing Lincoln he had the legal authority as president to use his war powers to free the slaves?

7. Where did Lincoln write the draft of the Emancipation Proclamation?

8. In whose desk did Lincoln keep his Emancipation Proclamation locked up while it was in work?

9. Who was the first person to read a draft of the Emancipation Proclamation?

10. On what occasion did Lincoln first mention to some of his cabinet members that he was seriously considering emancipation of the slaves?

11. When did Lincoln first make a formal announcement to his cabinet that he was going to free the slaves?

12. What suggestion did Seward make in regard to the timing of the Emancipation Proclamation?

13. What impact did the Emancipation Proclamation have on Great Britain's plans to intervene in the American Civil War?

14. What slaves did the preliminary Emancipation Proclamation declare to be free?

15. Why did Lincoln limit the Emancipation Proclamation's impact to slaves only in areas not yet occupied by Union forces?

✍ Emancipation (Answers)

1. It stated that when slaves were engaged in hostile military service, the owners' claims to the labor of such slaves were forfeited. But Union officers were reluctant to enforce it.

2. March 6, 1862.

3. Congress approved funding overwhelmingly, but none of the border state legislatures accepted it.

4. April 16, 1862.

5. During the early summer of 1862. He started writing a draft of the Emancipation Proclamation in early June.

6. *The War Powers of the President* by William Whiting. Charles Sumner gave him the book.

7. In the cipher room of the War Department. He had an officer keep it locked up in his desk, and worked on it for a period of at least two weeks.

8. Major Thomas T. Eckert's.

9. Vice President Hamlin, on June 18.

10. On July 13, 1862, while riding in a carriage with Seward and Welles, on the way to a funeral for Stanton's infant son.

11. On July 22, 1862. They were surprised, but generally supportive of the idea.

12. That Lincoln wait to issue it after a military victory, so that it wouldn't appear to be the "last measure of an exhausted government."

13. It caused the British prime minister to delay and, ultimately, abandon all idea of intervention.

14. Those in areas still in rebellion as of January 1, 1863.

15. Because in issuing the Emancipation Proclamation he was using his authority as commander in chief to remove slaves from the enemy. Legally, the Constitution would have to be amended to free slaves in those areas in loyal territory.

16. What were the political repercussions of the Emancipation Proclamation in the fall elections?

17. What was the Second Confiscation Act?

18. When was the Second Confiscation Act passed by Congress?

19. How many slaves were freed as a result of the Second Confiscation Act?

20. What was "The Prayer of Twenty Millions"?

21. How did Lincoln respond to Greeley's editorial, and what did he say?

22. Why didn't Lincoln admit that he had already planned on freeing the slaves when responding to Greeley's editorial?

23. What significant event took place at the White House on January 1, 1863?

24. What were two significant differences between the preliminary and the final Emancipation Proclamations?

25. In the 1863 annual message to Congress, what did Lincoln say about the future of the recently freed slaves?

26. How many slaves had been freed by the Emancipation Proclamation by February 1865?

27. What was the Freedman's Bureau Act?

16. The Republican Party lost a large number of congressional seats and governorships.

17. It was Congress's attempt to establish judicial means of confiscating the property, especially slaves, of those found guilty of insurrection. It was enforceable only through the courts, however, which proved an insufficient means in occupied Southern territory.

18. July 17, 1862.

19. According to Lincoln, zero. It was too difficult to use the civil courts to enforce this act.

20. An editorial by Horace Greeley of the New York *Tribune*, published on August 20, in which he pleaded with Lincoln to enforce the Second Confiscation Act and free the slaves.

21. He sent a letter, which was published in the *Tribune* on August 25. He responded that his "paramount" (not sole) object was to save the Union, rather than free the slaves. However, he hinted that he would do whatever was necessary in regards to freeing the slaves if he thought it would help save the Union.

22. He was waiting for a military victory and he wanted to assure everyone that freeing the slaves would be done for practical, as well as moral, reasons.

23. Lincoln signed the final Emancipation Proclamation, freeing the slaves in the states still in rebellion.

24. The final Emancipation Proclamation dropped the subject of colonizing African Americans, and it also allowed for enlistment of black troops.

25. He said that he would never allow them to be returned to slavery, and he would not attempt to retract or modify the Emancipation Proclamation. He said this in order to give a clear message to the opponents of the Emancipation Proclamation that were clamoring for its reversal.

26. Approximately 200,000. This was according to an estimate by William H. Seward.

27. A bill that gave Federal authorities guardianship over recently emancipated slaves. The act was to protect slaves from further exploitation by their former masters.

⚑ Foreign Relations

1. What foreign power sent its fleets to pay a friendly call at the North's Atlantic and Pacific ports in September 1863?

2. What was the name of the British ship that an American warship stopped and removed Southern diplomats from on November 8, 1861?

3. What was the name of the American ship that stopped the *Trent* and who was its commander?

4. What did Wilkes do and how was this an embarrassment to Lincoln?

5. Who were the Southern diplomats removed from the *Trent*?

6. What happened to Mason and Slidell?

7. What foreign leader offered to send Lincoln a stock of elephants to aid in the prosecution of the war effort?

8. What gifts did Lincoln accept from the King of Siam?

9. Shortly after Simon Cameron was appointed minister to Russia, he returned to the United States to run for the Senate. With whom did Lincoln replace him?

10. What British ship was involved in the second incident of a standoff with the British government over right of passage on the high seas?

11. What did Lincoln decide to do about the *Peterhoff?*

12. In the summer of 1862, which British leaders were leaning towards intervention in the American Civil War on behalf of the South?

13. Why did they abandon the idea?

14. What unexpected action did Horace Greeley of the New York *Tribune* take in regards to attempted mediation in the war effort in early 1863?

15. What group of British mill workers sent Lincoln an encouraging letter, praising the efforts of the American people and urging Lincoln to persevere?

✍ Foreign Relations (Answers)

1. Russia.

2. The *Trent.*

3. The USS *San Jacinto*, commanded by Captain Charles D. Wilkes.

4. He removed two Southern diplomats from the ship and brought them to the US, where they were jailed. This resulted in a protest from Great Britain and a threat of war with the United States.

5. James Mason of Virginia and John Slidell of Louisiana.

6. After a brief imprisonment at Fort Warren in Boston Harbor, Lincoln had them released, and they were allowed to go on to Great Britain. Their efforts to acquire Britain's diplomatic recognition of the Confederacy would eventually result in complete failure, however.

7. The King of Siam. Lincoln declined the offer with a gracious letter of thanks.

8. A photograph of the king, a sword, and elephant tusks.

9. Cassius Clay.

10. The *Peterhoff.* In early 1863 Union blockaders captured this British-owned merchant ship near Brownsville, Texas. His secretary of the navy, Gideon Welles, claimed the *Peterhoff* was carrying contraband, and the British claimed that international law had been violated by capturing the ship's mails.

11. Lincoln agreed with the British position and released the mails, diffusing a potentially explosive situation.

12. Prime Minister Lord Palmerston and British Foreign Secretary Earl Russell.

13. Because of the Union victory at Antietam and the Emancipation Proclamation.

14. He announced that the North was tired of the war and ready to restore "the Union as it was," meaning with slavery intact. He tried to enlist the French minister's aid to attain foreign intervention and convince Lincoln to cooperate, but Lincoln rejected the proposals.

15. The "Working Men of Manchester," England. Lincoln sent a noteworthy response, thanking them for their support.

⚑ The Gettysburg Address

1. What famous speech did Lincoln make on November 19, 1863, and what was the occasion?

2. How many words were in the Gettysburg Address?

3. Who was the famous orator that preceded Lincoln with a two-hour-long speech?

4. What did Everett talk about in his speech?

5. Did Lincoln's closing phrase "government of the people, by the people, and for the people" originate with the Gettysburg Address?

6. Is it true that Lincoln wrote the Gettysburg Address on the back of an envelope on the way to Gettysburg?

7. Who introduced Lincoln at Gettysburg?

8. How many times was Lincoln's address interrupted by applause from the audience?

9. What was the crowd's final reaction to the Gettysburg Address?

10. What distraction caused much of the crowd to laugh, rather than applaud, at the end of the address?

11. What were the newspapers' reactions to the Gettysburg Address?

12. What did the London *Times* say about the Gettysburg Address?

13. How did the Gettysburg Address illustrate the fact that Lincoln had transformed the war's purpose?

14. What sickness did Lincoln come down with during or soon after his trip to Gettysburg?

15. How long was Lincoln quarantined from visitors in the White House?

The Gettysburg Address (Answers)

1. His Gettysburg Address, delivered at the dedication of the soldiers' national cemetery.
2. Two hundred seventy-two.
3. Edward Everett, former United States senator and secretary of state.
4. He gave a detailed, memorized account of the battle that had taken place in July.
5. No. Theodore Parker's sermon entitled "The Effect of Slavery on the American People" used very similar words: "a government of all the people, by all the people, for all the people."
6. No. Lincoln took several weeks to prepare his address, but didn't actually make the last changes until the morning of the 19th.
7. Ward Lamon, master of ceremonies and long-time friend of Lincoln's.
8. Four times.
9. Most people were surprised that it ended so soon and it received little more than polite applause.
10. A photographer, who had thought he had plenty of time to photograph Lincoln, suddenly realized Lincoln had ended his speech and sat down before he could get his picture.
11. Generally very favorable. Many recognized it as a work of a skilled writer and statesman. Those newspapers that derided it were for the most part Democratic papers that rarely complimented anything Lincoln said or did.
12. The *Times* said, "the ceremony was rendered ludicrous by some of the sallies of that poor President Lincoln."
13. By referring to the Declaration of Independence, rather than the Constitution, Lincoln was able to declare that the war was for the purpose of "a new birth of freedom" for all men, as well as maintenance of democratic government.
14. Varioloid, which was a mild variant of smallpox.
15. Three weeks.

ﬧ Lincoln's Reelection

1. For what event did Lincoln seriously consider making a trip back to Springfield in early September 1863?

2. Did Lincoln attend the rally?

3. What concern of Lincoln's about Grant delayed his decision to bring the general east in order to take command of the Army of the Potomac?

4. Whom did Lincoln ask to inquire about Grant's political aspirations?

5. Was Grant interested in running for political office?

6. What political convention took place in Cleveland on May 31, 1864, and whom did they nominate for president?

7. How did Lincoln react to the news of the convention with four hundred dissatisfied Republicans?

8. Where was the convention that nominated Lincoln for president held in 1864, and on what dates?

9. In addition to being a Republican convention, how else did the Baltimore convention identify itself?

10. Was there any difficulty for Lincoln's supporters in obtaining the party's nomination for their chief in Baltimore?

11. To whom did the remaining 22 votes go?

12. What three men were considered for the vice presidential slot?

13. Whom did Lincoln prefer for the vice presidential position?

14. What was included in the National Union party's political platform regarding slavery?

15. In August 1864 a number of radical Republicans became interested in calling a second Republican convention in order to replace Lincoln as their presidential candidate. Where did they propose to hold the convention, and when?

16. Who was the radical Republicans' preferred replacement for Lincoln?

17. Whom did Lincoln send to visit Grant in order to find out if he was interested in the radicals' proposal of running him for president?

✍ Lincoln's Reelection (Answers)

1. A huge political rally "in favor of law and order and constitutional government." If he had gone, it would have essentially been for the purpose of kicking off his reelection campaign.

2. No. But he sent a carefully prepared letter, addressed to his friend James C. Conkling, which he asked to be read to the rally "very slowly."

3. He was concerned that Grant might want to run for president on the Republican ticket.

4. Elihu B. Washburne of Illinois, who knew Grant personally.

5. No. He was fully supportive of Lincoln.

6. In an effort to displace Lincoln as their party's nominee, a small group of about four hundred Republicans met in Cleveland to nominate John C. Fremont.

7. Amused, he picked up his Bible and read a passage from I Samuel that said, "and every one that was in distress, and every one that was in debt, and every one that was discontented, gathered themselves unto him; and he became a captain over them: and there were with him about four hundred men."

8. In Baltimore, on June 7–8, 1864. Baltimore was the same place the second Democratic convention had been held four years earlier, and had once been a beehive of secessionist sentiment.

9. As the convention of the National Union party. The intention was to appeal not only to Republicans, but to War Democrats as well.

10. No. Lincoln received 484 out of a possible 506 votes on the first ballot.

11. Grant. All of Grant's votes came from Missouri.

12. Vice President Hamlin, War Democrat Andrew Johnson of Tennessee, and Daniel S. Dickinson of New York.

13. Probably Hamlin, but he did not express his opinion publicly.

14. A call for an amendment to the Constitution abolishing slavery. Lincoln had strongly encouraged this.

15. In Cincinnati, on September 28.

16. Grant.

17. Colonel John Eaton.

18. What was Grant's response to Eaton when he was told that radical Republicans may be asking him to run for president?

19. In the summer of 1864, how did Lincoln respond to those that threatened to remove their political support of him if he didn't re-instate slavery?

20. Whom did the Democrats choose to run against Lincoln in the presidential race of 1864?

21. Was McClellan considered a "Peace" or "War" Democrat?

22. What military victory for the North had the effect of eliminating all serious opposition to Lincoln as the Republican Party nominee?

23. Which state's troops did Lincoln ask Sherman to furlough briefly so they could go home and vote in their state elections?

24. How did the soldier vote split between McClellan and Lincoln?

25. Which two great abolitionist leaders from the Massachusetts Anti-Slavery Society took opposing positions regarding Lincoln's re-election in 1864?

26. Did the black abolitionist Frederick Douglass support Lincoln's re-election?

27. Which of the two presidential candidates did most protestant religious groups support in the 1864 election?

28. Which presidential candidate did Ralph Waldo Emerson, Henry Wadsworth Longfellow, and Harriet Beecher Stowe support in the 1864 election?

29. How many states did Lincoln win in the presidential election?

30. How many votes did Lincoln win in the electoral college?

18. He said, "they can't do it! They can't compel me to do it!" Grant believed it was as important that Lincoln be reelected as it was that he defeat the Confederate armies.
19. He said that he would "be damned in time and eternity" if he returned blacks to slavery and allowed the South to keep its slaves. He pledged that "the world shall know that I will keep my faith to friends and enemies, come what will" and refused to back down from the abolition of slavery.
20. George B. McClellan.
21. War Democrat. But the platform he was given to run on was a "peace" platform, and he rejected many of its positions.
22. Sherman's taking of Atlanta on September 2, 1864. Suddenly Lincoln was popular again, among both Republicans and War Democrats.
23. Indiana's. Most states allowed their troops to vote in the field, but Indiana was an exception.
24. Lincoln received an overwhelming majority of the soldier vote, perhaps as much as 80 percent.
25. Wendell Phillips opposed Lincoln, and William Lloyd Garrison supported him.
26. Yes. He had initially favored Fremont, however.
27. Lincoln, by an overwhelming majority.
28. Lincoln.
29. All the Northern and border states except New Jersey, Kentucky, and Delaware—which went to McClellan.
30. Lincoln won 212 of 233 possible electoral votes.

⌘ Mary Lincoln in the White House

1. How much did Congress authorize to refurbish the White House in 1861?

2. How much did Mary Lincoln spend in refurbishing the White House?

3. Whom did Mary ask to tell Lincoln she had overrun the funds for refurbishment of the White House?

4. What was Lincoln's reaction when French told him he would have to ask for more money to cover the cost of the overruns?

5. How was the overrun finally taken care of?

6. When Willie died in February 1862, Mary was overcome by grief. How long was Mary bedridden after Willie's death?

7. What did Lincoln tell her might happen to her if she couldn't get control of her grief?

8. How long did Mary remain in mourning?

9. Who was Elizabeth Keckley and what was her association with Mary Lincoln?

10. What was the nickname Lincoln's secretaries Nicolay and Hay had for Mary Todd Lincoln?

11. Why was it Mary Todd Lincoln was sometimes referred to as a "traitor" by the press?

12. In the winter of 1863, Mary began consorting with what spiritualist in her effort to communicate with her dead sons?

13. On July 2, 1863, Mary was injured while taking a carriage ride. How was she hurt?

14. What relative of Mary's, who was the wife of a high ranking Confederate officer, lived in the White House for a week in December 1863?

15. What derogatory term did Mary Lincoln call U. S. Grant?

16. What luxuries did Mary buy in the fall of 1864, using credit and hiding the costs from Lincoln?

✒ Mary Lincoln in the White House (Answers)

1. $20,000, to be spent over a period of four years.
2. $26,700 in the first year.
3. Her friend Benjamin B. French, commissioner of public buildings.
4. Lincoln was furious, and said that he would never ask Congress for additional appropriations for "flub dubs for that damned old house!"
5. Congress quietly passed two deficiency appropriations to cover the overruns.
6. Three weeks. She did not attend the funeral, and frequently went into hysteric convulsions of grief.
7. He pointed to the mental hospital out the window and told her they might have to send her there if she didn't get better.
8. For well over a year. She wore black mourning dress until New Years' Day 1864.
9. A former slave that became Mrs. Lincoln's seamstress and closest confidante while in the White House.
10. "The Hellcat."
11. Several of her half brothers from Kentucky had joined the Confederate army.
12. Nettie Colburn. She held several séances in the White House. Mary told Lincoln that Willie came to her bedside every night.
13. She was thrown from the carriage and hit her head on a sharp rock. The wound became infected, and it took weeks for her to recover. Afterwards her headaches became more frequent and her son Robert would later say she never fully recovered from her fall.
14. Emilie Todd Helm, wife of Confederate General Benjamin Hardin Helm. General Helm had been killed in the Battle of Chickamauga, and the Lincolns allowed her to visit with them for a week before it became politically embarrassing and she had to leave.
15. A butcher. Mary, like many people, thought Grant careless in the way he threw men into battle.
16. Jewelry and clothing. She hoped that Lincoln would be re-elected so that her creditors would not require immediate payment. She feared that if Lincoln lost, her creditors would demand payment and her husband would find out about her extravagances.

17. How long was Mary bedridden after Lincoln was assassinated?

18. Where did Mary and her sons move to after they left the White House?

17. For a month. It was over a month before she moved out of the White House.
18. Chicago.

Lincoln and the Press

1. What were the "Sampson's Ghost" letters?
2. What Chicago newspaper editor was a staunch supporter of Lincoln's efforts in his 1858 Senate campaign?
3. Who published the first biographical sketch of Lincoln?
4. What was the Republican newspaper of Springfield that supported Lincoln's candidacy?
5. Who was the editor of the *Illinois State Journal*?
6. What German-American newspaper did Lincoln secretly purchase on May 30, 1859?
7. How much did he pay for the *Staats-Anzeiger*?
8. How long did Lincoln retain ownership of the German paper?
9. What was Lincoln's first connection with John G. Nicolay, his future secretary in the White House?
10. What newspapers published on May 18, 1864, a false proclamation, purportedly by Lincoln, that called for an additional 400,000 men to be drafted?
11. What two men fabricated the draft proclamation and why?
12. What punitive measures did the Lincoln administration impose on the newspapers and reporters responsible?
13. To what New York editor did Lincoln offer the position of minister to France if he would drop his vindictive attacks on the Lincoln administration?
14. Who was the eccentric editor of the nation's most powerful newspaper, *The New York Tribune*?

✍ Lincoln and the Press (Answers)

1. Several anonymous letters Lincoln had published in the *Sangamo Journal* newspaper in 1842, attacking a prominent Democratic office holder over land fraud.

2. Charles H. Ray of the Chicago *Press and Tribune.*

3. Joseph Lewis of the *Chester County (Pennsylvania) Times.* Lincoln provided the material for this through an intermediary, Jesse W. Fell, of Bloomington, Illinois.

4. The *Illinois State Journal.*

5. Edward L. Baker.

6. The Springfield Illinois' *Staats-Anzeiger.* Theodore Canisius was the editor.

7. $400.

8. Eighteen months. He sold it to Canisius on December 6, 1860.

9. He offered Nicolay $500 to promote the circulation of the St. Louis *Democrat*, a Republican paper, in southern Illinois. Nicolay was a newspaperman and German-American.

10. The New York *World* and the *Journal of Commerce.*

11. Joseph Howard, an editor of the Brooklyn *Daily Eagle*, and Francis A. Mallison, a reporter of the same. They were speculating in the gold market and hoped to benefit from the rise in gold prices.

12. They shut down the newspapers for two days and temporarily incarcerated the editors and proprietors. Howard and Mallison were imprisoned in Fort Lafayette.

13. James Gordon Bennett of the New York *Herald.* Bennett did not endorse either Lincoln or McClellan. Lincoln offered him the ministry to France, though, in spite of the fact he knew Bennett would refuse it.

14. Horace Greeley.

Life in the White House

1. What bank did Lincoln use while president?
2. During Lincoln's first months in the White House, what was the name of the old Irish doorkeeper whose duty was to keep out unwanted visitors?
3. While living in the White House, what did Lincoln typically have for breakfast?
4. What two men's portraits hung on Lincoln's study walls?
5. Who were Lincoln's secretaries while in the White House?
6. How many letters did Lincoln receive each day?
7. What were Nicolay and Hay's nicknames for Lincoln?
8. Why did they call him the "Tycoon"?
9. What were the personal relationships between Lincoln and his secretaries?
10. How often did Lincoln receive the general public in the White House?
11. What did Lincoln call these visits with the people?
12. Where did the Lincolns live during the summer while in Washington?

✍ Life in the White House (Answers)

1. Riggs and Company in Washington, D.C.
2. Edward McManus—who rarely kept out anyone that was really determined to see the president.
3. A cup of coffee and an egg.
4. President Andrew Jackson and John Bright, the English Liberal Leader.
5. John G. Nicolay, John Hay, William O. Stoddard, Edward D. Neill, John George, and William Osborn. There were typically only two or three on the payroll at a time.
6. Two to three hundred. His secretaries would screen them to see whether or not the president needed to respond. They also disposed of the threatening letters.
7. The "Ancient" and the "Tycoon."
8. A term of respect, in reference to the all-powerful Emperor of Japan.
9. Both Nicolay and Hay admired Lincoln. Lincoln called Hay "John" and treated him almost like a son. Nicolay, who was older, Lincoln called by his last name and treated him with more respect.
10. Typically at least three days a week, beginning at 10:00 A.M. and sometimes lasting for several hours.
11. His "public opinion baths."
12. In the US Soldiers' Home, near the present-day Veterans Administration Hospital.

🏳 Guarding Lincoln

1. What were the security arrangements at the White House at the outbreak of the war?

2. In late 1861, how was security improved at the White House?

3. What changes were made to the White House security in the summer of 1863?

4. How did the chief of the Washington Metropolitan Police Department help improve White House security?

5. In August 1864, someone took a shot at Lincoln one evening when he was riding a horse returning to the Soldiers' Home. How close did the shot come?

6. In September 1864, what Confederate spy came through the Union lines, along with three associates, in an attempt to capture Lincoln on the grounds of the Soldiers' Home in Washington?

7. What happened when Conrad tried to capture Lincoln?

✍ Guarding Lincoln (Answers)

1. There were two unarmed civilian attendants—one for the outer door and one for the president's office door. Lincoln usually went unescorted when he left the White House.

2. Company K of the 100th Pennsylvania "Bucktails" was assigned to guard the gates and doors.

3. The Union Light Guard, a company of one hundred Ohioans was detailed to White House security. Two of these guards were stationed at all times at each of the gateways to the White House.

4. Beginning in November 1864, he detailed four (later supplemented by seven more) officers that wore civilian clothing and carried concealed weapons. They were to accompany Lincoln on walks, trips to the theater, and remain on duty outside of Lincoln's bedroom.

5. Close enough that Lincoln's horse bolted, causing him to lose his hat. His hat was retrieved later. Historians debate whether or not the shot actually went through his hat, as some accounts claim.

6. Thomas Nelson Conrad, a Confederate minister of the Gospel.

7. He found Lincoln too heavily guarded. He remained in Washington until early November, and finally gave up.

♭ Second Inaugural Address

1. How many words were in Lincoln's Second Inaugural Address?
2. What did Lincoln say, in his Second Inaugural Address, the cause of the war had been?
3. Why did Lincoln say, in his Second Inaugural Address, the war had gone on for so long?
4. What are the famous closing lines of the Second Inaugural Address?
5. How many references to God are there in the Second Inaugural Address?
6. How many direct quotations of the Bible are in the Second Inaugural Address?
7. What scripture is quoted?
8. What was Lincoln's own opinion of his Second Inaugural Address?
9. What did Frederick Douglass call Lincoln's Second Inaugural Address?
10. What happened to Lincoln's original handwritten copy of the Second Inaugural Address?

✍ Second Inaugural Address (Answers)

1. Seven hundred three. It was the shortest Inaugural Address written up to that time.

2. Slavery.

3. Because "God wills that it continue" until all the "blood drawn with the lash" (slavery) be paid for by blood "drawn by the sword."

4. "With malice toward none; with charity for all; with firmness in the right, as God gives us to see the right, let us strive on to finish the work we are in; to bind up the nation's wounds; to care for him who shall have borne the battle, and for his widow, and his orphan—to do all which may achieve and cherish a just, and a lasting peace, among ourselves, and with all nations."

5. Fourteen.

6. Four.

7. Genesis 3:19, Matthew 7:1, Matthew 18:7, Psalm 19:9.

8. "Lots of wisdom in that document, I suspect." He thought it would "wear as well" as anything he'd written.

9. "A sacred effort."

10. Lincoln gave it to this secretary John Hay on April 10, 1865. His heirs subsequently donated it to the Library of Congress.

Peace Efforts

1. What two men did Lincoln send to Niagara Falls in mid-July 1864 to meet with three representatives of the Confederate government regarding possible peace terms?

2. What were the names of the Confederate emissaries that met with Greeley and Hay?

3. What two terms did Lincoln tell them he required for peace?

4. What was Jefferson Davis' reaction to these terms?

5. What Confederate peace commissioners did Lincoln and William H. Seward meet at Hampton Roads, Virginia, on February 3, 1865?

6. Did they come to any agreeable solution for peace?

7. What was Lincoln's comment when he saw the 90-pound Stephens remove his huge overcoat and several shawls before sitting down to the conference table?

🖎 Peace Efforts (Answers)

1. John Hay, Lincoln's secretary, and Horace Greeley, editor of the New York *Tribune*. Greeley was sent because he had insisted that Lincoln communicate with the Confederates.
2. Alabama Senator Clement C. Clay, former Mississippi Congressman Jacob Thompson, and Professor James P. Holcombe of the University of Virginia.
3. The "integrity of the whole Union and abandonment of slavery."
4. He rejected them, insisting on the independence of the Confederate States.
5. Alexander Stephens, vice president of the Confederate States; John A. Hunter, Confederate assistant secretary of war; and Robert M. T. Hunter, a Confederate senator from Virginia.
6. No. Lincoln insisted on the Confederate States' return to the Union, and they wanted to maintain independence.
7. "Never have I seen so small a nubbin come out of so much husk."

♔ John Wilkes Booth

1. Had Lincoln ever seen the actor John Wilkes Booth perform?

2. What was the primary topic of Lincoln's last public speech, made from a White House second-story window on April 11?

3. What famous actor was in the crowd, listening to Lincoln's speech?

4. What did Lincoln say in his speech that caused Booth to swear that it would be "the last speech he will ever make"?

5. Where was John Wilkes Booth from?

6. Who else in Booth's family were actors?

7. Did Booth's family share his sympathy with the South?

8. Why did Booth hate Lincoln?

9. What scheme did Booth propose to the Confederate Secret Service regarding Lincoln?

10. Did any high-level Confederate officials approve of Booth's plan?

11. What were the names of the men Booth enlisted in his capture scheme?

12. When was Booth's first plan to capture Lincoln to take place?

13. What was his second plan to capture Lincoln?

14. When did Booth start thinking about assassinating Lincoln instead of capturing him?

15. When did Booth finally decide to kill Lincoln?

✍ John Wilkes Booth (Answers)

1. Yes. In the play "The Marble Heart."
2. Reconstruction of the South.
3. John Wilkes Booth.
4. He proposed that some of the blacks be given the right to vote.
5. Bel Air, Maryland. He was the next-to-the-youngest of 10 children.
6. His father, Junius Brutus Booth, and brothers Edwin and Junius Brutus, Jr. All four men were talented Shakespearean actors, and John Wilkes had a repertoire of nine Shakespearean leading roles.
7. No.
8. He considered him uncouth and was particularly angered by Lincoln's attack on slavery.
9. That he and some fellow conspirators capture Lincoln and take him south to be exchanged for Confederate prisoners.
10. There is no conclusive evidence that any high-level government official approved of Booth's scheme to capture Lincoln.
11. Samuel B. Arnold, Michael O'Laughlin, George A. Atzerodt, John H. Surratt, Lewis Thornton Powell (alias Paine), David E. Herold, and Thomas Harbin.
12. On January 18, 1865, at Ford's Theatre. Booth developed a scheme that called for him and his associates to capture Lincoln during a play and take him across the stage to an awaiting carriage.
13. To capture him while he was on his way back from a performance of "Still Waters Run Deep" at the Campbell Hospital, near the Soldiers' Home, on March 17, 1865. Lincoln didn't go to the play that evening.
14. Somewhere between late March and April 11.
15. While listening to him make his April 11 speech from the White House window. He urged his companion, Powell, to shoot him on the spot, but Powell refused.

⚑ Lincoln Goes to Richmond

1. On what date did Lincoln and Tad visit Richmond?
2. How did Lincoln get to Richmond?
3. How was Lincoln escorted as he walked through Richmond?
4. Where did Lincoln go while visiting Richmond?
5. What did Lincoln ask for when he sat down at Jefferson Davis' desk?
6. What Confederate official did Lincoln meet while in the Confederate White House?
7. Who, in addition to Campbell, met with Lincoln on April 5?
8. What proposition did Lincoln make to Campbell and Myers regarding the Virginia legislature?
9. Although most residents of Richmond resented Lincoln's presence in the city, some were ecstatic to see him. Who were they?
10. What official from Lincoln's cabinet was injured in a carriage accident while Lincoln was in Richmond?
11. What reconstruction idea did Lincoln present to his cabinet on April 12?

✍ Lincoln Goes to Richmond (Answers)

1. April 4, 1865. Jefferson Davis and the Confederate government had abandoned it two days earlier.

2. In a barge rowed by 12 sailors.

3. Initially, he was protected only by the 12 sailors armed with carbines. Later, they were joined by a squad of soldiers.

4. To the Confederate White House, where Jefferson Davis had lived.

5. A glass of water.

6. John A. Campbell, one of the Southern commissioners at the Hampton Roads conference. Lincoln talked briefly with Campbell and asked him to bring other Virginia state leaders to a conference the next day.

7. Gustavus A. Myers, a prominent Richmond attorney. The other leaders Campbell invited declined to accompany him.

8. That they be given safe conduct to Richmond in order to vote and withdraw the state from the Confederacy. They eagerly accepted this idea, but took so long in arranging it that Lincoln was dead before anything happened.

9. The slaves.

10. Secretary of State William H. Seward. His arm and jaw were broken, and he was confined to bed rest.

11. The assembly of the Virginia legislature idea he had proposed to Cambell on April 5. His cabinet made effective arguments against it, and Lincoln decided to drop it.

Lincoln's Physical and Personal Characteristics

1. How tall was Lincoln?
2. How much did he weigh when he became president?
3. What disease has been proposed as a possible cause of Lincoln's extreme height?
4. What was Lincoln's dominant psychological trait?
5. How did Lincoln cope with melancholia and depression?
6. What did Lincoln call his melancholia?
7. What sciences did Lincoln take particular interest in?
8. Did Lincoln drink or smoke?
9. Did Lincoln swear?
10. What name did Lincoln prefer to be called?
11. What was Lincoln's favorite song?
12. What was Lincoln's hat size?
13. What was Lincoln's favorite Shakespearean play?
14. What was Lincoln's favorite line from Shakespeare?
15. What were Lincoln's favorite forms of recreation while president?
16. What was Lincoln's shoe size?

✍ Lincoln's Physical and Personal Characteristics (Answers)

1. Six feet, four inches.
2. About 180 pounds.
3. Marfan syndrome. This is still debated, however.
4. Melancholia.
5. Humor. He used jokes and funny stories to help cheer himself up.
6. "Hypo." This was short for hypochondria.
7. Astronomy and mechanics.
8. No.
9. He very rarely used profane language in anger. He would occasionally use profanity when telling a joke, however.
10. He preferred simply "Lincoln." He did not like to be called Abe, Abraham, or "Old Abe."
11. Not known. Robert Lincoln said that he never heard his father state what song was his favorite, although it is known he was very fond of *The Battle Hymn of the Republic, Your Mission*, the *Marseillaise*, and *The Soldier's Chorus*.
12. Seven and one eighth.
13. Macbeth.
14. "Oh my offence is rank" from Hamlet.
15. The theatre and carriage rides with Mary.
16. Fourteen.

ꕔ Trivial

1. What was Lincoln's annual salary as president?
2. What was the Treasury Note Bill and when did Lincoln sign it?
3. Who were two of Lincoln's favorite humorists?
4. What was Lincoln's peculiar manner of reading newspapers?
5. What was the first town to be named after Lincoln, and when did this take place?
6. What did Lincoln say to the fathers when he was told what they planned to name the town?
7. What Springfield resident did Lincoln entrust with his financial affairs when he left for Washington, D.C.?
8. How many times did President Lincoln pardon offenders convicted by civil courts?
9. What African American did Lincoln call "one of the most meritorious men in America"?
10. What song did Lincoln describe as "one of the best tunes I ever heard."
11. What is the historical significance of Lincoln's proclamation of Thanksgiving for the last day of November 1863?
12. Who inspired Lincoln to make the November 1863 proclamation of Thanksgiving?
13. What was the "Bixby Letter"?
14. Had Mrs. Bixby, in fact, lost five sons in the war?
15. Where is the original copy of the Bixby Letter?
16. There has been a debate among historians, some proposing that the Bixby Letter was not written by Lincoln, but by whom?
17. What Democratic politician did Ambrose Burnside, who had been appointed commander of the Department of Ohio, arrest on May 6 for making disloyal speeches and supporting the Confederacy?
18. What happened to Vallandigham after his arrest?

✍ Trivial (Answers)

1. $25,000.

2. Also called the Legal Tender Act, it provided for the issuance of a national paper currency in lieu of coin. Lincoln signed it on February 25, 1862.

3. Orpheus C. Kerr and Artemus Ward.

4. He would lay on the couch and read them out loud. He said that he retained what he read this way because "two senses catch the idea."

5. The capital of Logan County, Illinois, was named after Lincoln on February 12, 1853. Lincoln was a lawyer at the time and had been retained by the city fathers to draw up the bill creating the town.

6. "Anything named Lincoln never amounted to much."

7. Robert Irwin, cashier at the Springfield Marine and Fire Insurance Company. Irwin took care of Lincoln's finances until he died a month before Lincoln was assassinated in 1865.

8. Three hundred seventy-five times. These were for various crimes, such as larceny, manslaughter, and embezzlement.

9. Frederick Douglass.

10. "Dixie."

11. This was the first of the annual proclamations for a national Thanksgiving Day that has continued ever since. Prior to Lincoln's proclamation, days of Thanksgiving were sporadic or nonnational in scope.

12. Sarah Josepha Hale, editor of *Godey's Lady's Book*.

13. A letter of condolence written by Lincoln to a widow that had purportedly lost five sons, fighting for the Union.

14. No. Two had been killed in combat, one had been honorably discharged, one deserted, and one either deserted or died a prisoner of war.

15. It was lost and has never been found. Numerous facsimiles have been created, imitating Lincoln's handwriting, but the only real account of what the letter said is from contemporary newspaper accounts that reprinted the text in full.

16. Lincoln's secretary John Hay.

17. Clement L. Vallandigham.

18. Initially sentenced to prison by a military tribunal, Lincoln had him banished to the South instead. Lincoln, who had not known about the arrest until he learned of it in the newspapers, regretted Burnside's action, as it had severe impact on the Democratic Party support to Lincoln's policies.

19. What did Ohio Democrats do to show their disapproval of the Lincoln administration's actions regarding Vallandigham?
20. What did Lincoln get a patent for on May 22, 1849?
21. What was Lincoln's patent number?
22. What did Lincoln say was "the best speech he ever heard"?
23. How many justices did Lincoln appoint to the Supreme Court?
24. Did Lincoln ever own slaves?
25. Was Lincoln a Free Mason?
26. Where did Lincoln frequently store important papers?
27. What theatres did the Lincolns attend in Washington?
28. What was the last song Lincoln heard before he died?
29. Where did Lincoln tell Mary he wanted to travel to after he was done with his second term of office?
30. Where did he tell Mary he wanted to move after they left the White House?
31. Did Lincoln have a will?
32. Who handled Lincoln's finances and was administrator of estate after his assassination?
33. What was Lincoln's financial worth in 1860?
34. What was the net value of Lincoln's estate at Lincoln's death?
35. What was the net value of the estate when it was divided in November 1867?
36. How was Lincoln's estate divided?
37. What did Davis charge for his administrator services?
38. What were the contents of Lincoln's pockets the night he was assassinated?

19. They nominated him for governor, even though he was in exile.
20. A device to lift boats over shoals. Lincoln is the only US president to have ever obtained a patent.
21. 6649.
22. Daniel Webster's "Second reply to Hayne."
23. Five. Chief Justice Salmon P. Chase, Justice David Davis, Justice Stephen J. Field, Justice Noah Swayne, and Justice Samuel F. Miller.
24. No. His father-in-law did, however.
25. No. Lincoln did not belong to any secret or religious societies.
26. In his hat.
27. Grover's Theatre on E Street and Ford's Theatre on Tenth Street.
28. *"Hail to the Chief"* when he entered Ford's Theatre.
29. First to Europe, and then to California.
30. He was not certain.
31. No. He died intestate.
32. Supreme Court Justice David Davis.
33. He owned real estate valued at $5,000 and a personal estate of $12,000.
34. $83,343.70.
35. $110,974.62, excluding real estate. Davis, through wise investment, had increased it over $27,000.
36. Mary, Robert, and Tad each received a third.
37. Nothing. He was entitled to $6,600.
38. Two pairs of spectacles and cases, a lens polisher, a cuff button, a pocketknife, a watch fob, a linen handkerchief, a brown leather wallet containing a five-dollar Confederate note and nine newspaper clippings.

◫ Last Day

1. What Union general participated in Lincoln's final cabinet meeting on April 14?
2. During the final cabinet meeting, why did Lincoln say he believed they would soon receive good news about the surrender of the Confederate army facing Sherman in North Carolina?
3. What happened in Lincoln's dream?
4. On what other occasions had Lincoln had the dream?
5. What recreation did Lincoln enjoy on the afternoon of April 14?
6. Were Lincoln and Mary guarded during their carriage ride?
7. What military institution did Mary and Lincoln visit during their last carriage ride together?
8. What did Lincoln tell Mary the significance of April 14 was?
9. What is the last thing written by Lincoln?
10. Who was the last person to call on Lincoln before he went to Ford's Theatre, and what did Lincoln say to him?

✍ Last Day (Answers)

1. General U. S. Grant.

2. Lincoln said he had a dream the previous night, similar to one that he'd had previously that always preceded good news.

3. He was on the water, in some "singular, indescribable vessel, and . . . he was moving with great rapidity towards an indefinite shore."

4. Before nearly every important Union victory: Antietam, Gettysburg, Stones River, Vicksburg, and Fort Fisher.

5. He and Mary went on a final carriage ride through south Washington.

6. Yes. Cavalrymen rode behind the barouche.

7. The Navy Yard. Lincoln made a brief visit to the monitor *Montauk*.

8. He considered that as of that day, the war had come to a close. He was very lighthearted, and told her that both of them needed to be more cheerful in the future.

9. "Allow Mr. Ashmun & friend to come in at 9. A.M. to-morrow." This was written shortly after 8:00 p.m., just as Lincoln was getting ready to leave for Ford's Theatre.

10. Congressman Isaac N. Arnold. As Lincoln was getting into the carriage, he told him to come and see him in the morning.

🔖 The Assassination

1. What were the names of the nine people Lincoln invited to accompany him and Mary to Ford's Theatre the evening of April 14, before getting acceptance by a young officer and his fiancée?
2. Who accompanied the Lincolns to Ford's Theatre?
3. What was the name of the play the Lincolns saw at Ford's Theatre?
4. What were the last words Lincoln heard before being shot?
5. Whom besides Lincoln, did Booth plan on assassinating the night of April 14?
6. Whom did Booth assign to kill Johnson and Seward?
7. Booth wrote a letter explaining his reasons for killing Lincoln to what newspaper?
8. Why was Booth able to gain access to Lincoln's theatre box so easily?
9. What were the names of the valet and the policeman that had left his post?
10. How close did Booth get to Lincoln before shooting him?
11. What type of weapon did Booth use?
12. Where did Booth shoot the president?
13. What time was it when Lincoln was shot?
14. What did Booth do after shooting Lincoln?
15. What happened to Booth when he landed on the stage?
16. What did Booth shout to the crowd when he stood up on the stage?
17. Who was the first doctor to reach the president?
18. What medical treatment did Leale administer to Lincoln?
19. Who was the second doctor to arrive?

✍ The Assassination (Answers)

1. Mr. and Mrs. Edwin Stanton, General and Mrs. Grant, Governor Oglesby and General Haynie, a Detroit paymaster by the name of Howard, William H. Wallace, and Major Thomas Eckert.

2. Major Henry R. Rathbone and his fiancée, Clara Harris.

3. *Our American Cousin*, starring the actress Laura Keene.

4. The lines of the character Asa Trenchard, who said, "Don't know the manners of good society, eh? Well, I guess I know enough to turn you inside out, old gal—you sockdologizing old man-trap."

5. Vice President Andrew Johnson and Secretary of State William H. Seward.

6. Atzerodt was to kill Johnson, and Powell to kill Seward. All three assaults were to take place at 10:15 P.M.

7. The *National Intelligencer*. The letter was never received by the newspaper, however, because the friend Booth entrusted it to read it and destroyed it.

8. The Washington Metropolitan policeman assigned to protect the president had left his post, and Lincoln's personal valet that remained outside the box allowed Booth in when he showed him his calling card.

9. The valet was Charles Forbes, and the policeman was John Parker.

10. He was about two feet away.

11. A single-shot derringer.

12. In the back of the head.

13. Between 10:15 and 10:20 P.M.

14. First, he struggled with Major Rathbone, who was trying to subdue him. After cutting the arm of Rathbone with his knife, he jumped from the box to the stage.

15. He broke his left leg. He had caught the spur of his heel in the flags decorating the presidential box, and landed on one foot, breaking the bone just above the ankle.

16. "Sic semper tyrannis!" the motto of the State of Virginia. Some people thought he shouted, "The South is avenged!"

17. Army surgeon Charles A. Leale.

18. After stretching him out on the floor of the box, he removed a clot of blood from the wound and then administered artificial respiration. This started Lincoln breathing again.

19. Charles S. Taft, brother of Julia Taft who had babysat the Lincoln boys in the White House. Both had been in the audience during the play.

20. Where did they move Lincoln to?
21. What did they do when they found the bed at the Petersen home was too short for Lincoln?
22. How many doctors attended Lincoln between the time of the shooting and his death the next morning?
23. What were the doctors' names?
24. Did Lincoln ever regain consciousness after being shot?
25. When Robert Lincoln arrived at the Petersen house and saw how distraught his mother was, whom did he ask to come and comfort her?
26. Which of Lincoln's cabinet members came to see their dying chief at the Petersen house?
27. How was Seward wounded by Powell?
28. Was Vice President Johnson attacked?
29. What minister of the Gospel came to the Petersen house?
30. At what time did Lincoln die?
31. What were the famous words of tribute Stanton said of Lincoln shortly after he died?
32. When was Booth captured?
33. Who killed John Wilkes Booth?
34. How many people were tried in the assassination plot and what happened to each of them?
35. Where was Booth's body buried?

20. Across the street, to the home of a merchant-tailor, William Petersen.

21. They placed him diagonally across it.

22. Fourteen.

23. Charles Leale, Charles Taft, C. D. Gatch, Albert F. King, Surgeon General Joseph Barnes, Assistant Surgeon General Charles H. Crane, Surgeon D. Willard Bliss, Ezra W. Abbott, C. H. Lieberman, J. C. Hall, S. T. Ford, William B. Notson, Dr. J. F. May, Dr. Stone.

24. No.

25. A close friend of Mary's, Elizabeth Dixon, wife of Connecticut Senator James Dixon.

26. All of them, except Seward, who had been attacked by Powell.

27. Powell had broken into his room, where Seward was still bedridden from the carriage accident, and attacked him with a knife. Seward survived, but was seriously wounded.

28. No. Atzerodt lost his nerve and did not attempt to attack Johnson.

29. Phineas D. Gurley, pastor of the New York Avenue Presbyterian Church, the church the Lincolns frequently attended.

30. At 7:22 A.M. on the morning of April 15.

31. "Now he belongs to the ages."

32. The morning of April 26, when he and Herold were found in a barn near Port Royal, Virginia. When Booth refused to come out, the barn was fired, and he was subsequently shot by one of the cavalrymen.

33. New York cavalryman Thomas P. Corbett. Corbett, a hatter by trade, was later committed to an insane asylum.

34. Eight. Samuel Arnold was condemned to life imprisonment at hard labor. He was pardoned in 1869 by President Johnson. George Atzerodt was hanged. Booth was shot by Federal cavalry when he refused to surrender. David Herold was hanged. Dr. Samuel Mudd was condemned to life imprisonment at hard labor, then pardoned in 1869 by President Johnson. Michael O'Laughlin was sentenced to life imprisonment at hard labor, and died at Fort Jefferson of yellow fever in 1867. Lewis Powell was hanged. Mary Surratt was hanged. The (separate) trial of John Surratt, who had gone into hiding, ended in a hung jury and subsequently nolle prosequi.

35. Initially, at the Washington Arsenal. It was later transferred to Green Mount Cemetery in Baltimore.

ꇙ Lincoln's Descendants

1. When did Tad Lincoln die, and from what cause?
2. In what year was Mary Lincoln committed to an insane asylum?
3. Who had her committed?
4. How long was Mary in the insane asylum?
5. Where did Mary live during the last year of her life?
6. When did Mary Todd Lincoln die?
7. What did Robert do, professionally?
8. What were Robert's hobbies?
9. In what year did Robert Todd Lincoln die?
10. When did Robert Lincoln's wife, Mary, die?
11. What were the names of Robert Todd Lincoln's children?
12. What happened to Robert's son, Abraham?
13. What happened to Robert's daughter, Mary, and her descendants?
14. What happened to Jessie Lincoln and her descendants?
15. When did the last direct descendant of Abraham Lincoln die?

✍ Lincoln's Descendants (Answers)

1. On July 15, 1871, of tuberculosis. He was 17 years old.
2. 1875.
3. Her son, Robert.
4. About four months. Afterwards she went to Europe until 1880.
5. At her sister's, the Edwards home in Springfield. She stayed in a room with the shades drawn and dimly lit by candles.
6. July 16, 1882.
7. He was a lawyer, the secretary of war under President Arthur, the minister to England for President Harrison, and the president of the Pullman Palace (railroad) Car Company.
8. Golf and astronomy.
9. 1926.
10. 1937.
11. Mary (b. 1869), Abraham (b. 1873), and Jessie (b. 1875).
12. He died at the age of 17 of blood poisoning.
13. Mary married Charles Bradley Isham, and they had one son, Lincoln Isham, who died in 1971, childless. Mary died in 1938.
14. Jessie married Warren Wallace Beckwith and had two children, Mary Lincoln Beckwith and Robert Lincoln Beckwith. Mary Lincoln Beckwith never married. Her brother Robert Lincoln Beckwith (b. 1904) was married twice but had no children and became the last direct descendant of Abraham Lincoln. Jessie Lincoln died in 1948.
15. Robert Lincoln Beckwith died in 1985.

♖ Memorials and Memorabilia

1. When was the Lincoln penny first issued?
2. What was the controversy that first raged over the Lincoln penny?
3. What are the Lincoln papers?
4. When were the Lincoln papers made available to the public?
5. When was the Lincoln Memorial in Washington, D.C. dedicated?
6. Who was the memorial's architect?
7. Who was the sculptor of the memorial's Lincoln statue?
8. What two changes did French make to the original plan for the statue?
9. How much did the Lincoln Memorial cost?
10. What changes did French require of the lighting in the memorial after it was finished?
11. How many columns are in the Lincoln Memorial and what does each column represent?
12. Where is Lincoln buried?
13. Who designed the Lincoln Tomb at Oak Ridge?
14. In how many places were Lincoln's remains buried before being permanently interred in the Lincoln Tomb at Oak Ridge?
15. What bizarre plot involving Lincoln's remains was discovered by detectives in 1876?
16. Did the grave robbers succeed?
17. What were the names of the robbers?
18. Who was the secret service agent that infiltrated the Kinealy gang and uncovered the plot?
19. What happened to the grave robbers?
20. What college conferred on Lincoln an LL.D. degree?
21. What was the earliest campaign biography of Lincoln to be published?
22. What was the most widely distributed of the early Lincoln biographies?

✍ Memorials and Memorabilia (Answers)

1. August 2, 1909.

2. The Lincoln penny was the first to have the likeness of an American president engraved on it. Critics thought that engraving the heads of state on coins to be a monarchical practice.

3. A large collection of letters written to Lincoln, most of them during his presidency. They are currently in the Library of Congress.

4. July 26, 1947, 21 years after Robert Lincoln's death.

5. May 30, 1922.

6. Henry Bacon.

7. William Chester French.

8. He changed it from bronze to marble and increased its height from 12 feet to 19.

9. Three million dollars.

10. He arranged to have artificial lighting added in the ceiling. This was because he was dissatisfied with the way the light from the front illuminated Lincoln's face.

11. Thirty-six. The number of states in the Union at the time of Lincoln's death.

12. In Oak Ridge Cemetery in Springfield, Illinois.

13. Larkin G. Mead, a sculptor from Brattleboro, Vermont.

14. Six.

15. A plot to steal his corpse by thieves that wanted to exchange it for the release of counterfeiter Benjamin Boyd from prison.

16. No. They were stopped before they could remove the coffin from the sarcophagus.

17. Jim Kinealy, Terrence Mullen, and John Hughes.

18. Lewis G. Swegles.

19. They were sentenced to a year in prison.

20. Knox College.

21. "Life, Speeches, and Public Services of Abram. Lincoln, Together with a Sketch of the Life of Hannibal Hamlin," which was issued in "The Wigwam Edition" by Rudd and Carleton of New York on June 2, 1860.

22. Life of Lincoln by John Locke Scripps, editor of the Chicago *Press and Tribune*.

Bibliography

Angle, Paul M., and Earl Schenck Miers, eds. *Fire the Salute! Abe Lincoln is Nominated! Murat Halstead Reports the Republican National Convention in Chicago May 16, 17, & 18, 1860.* Kingsport, Tenn.: Kingsport Press.

Barton, William. *The Lineage of Lincoln.* Indianapolis: Bobbs-Merrill, 1929.

Basler, Roy P., ed., Marion Dolores Pratt and Lloyd A. Dunlap, asst. eds. *The Collected Works of Abraham Lincoln.* New Brunswick, N.J.: Rutgers University Press, 1955.

Beveridge, Albert J. *Abraham Lincoln 1809–1858*, 2 vols. New York: Houghton Mifflin Company, 1928.

Bishop, Jim. *The Day Lincoln Was Shot.* New York: Harper and Brothers, 1955.

Brooks, Noah. *Washington in Lincoln's Time.* H. Mitgang, ed. New York: Rinehart and Company, 1958.

Bruce, Robert V. *Lincoln and the Tools of War.* Urbana, Ill.: University of Illinois Press, 1989.

Burlingame, Michael. *The Inner World of Abraham Lincoln.* Urbana, Ill.: University of Illinois Press, 1994.

———. *An Oral History of Abraham Lincoln: John G. Nicolay's Interviews and Essays.* Carbondale: Southern Illinois University Press, 1996.

Carpenter, F. B. *The Inner Life of Abraham Lincoln.* Boston: Houghton, Mifflin & Co., 1883.

Donald, David H. *Lincoln.* New York: Touchstone, 1996.

Duff, John J. *Abraham Lincoln, Prairie Lawyer.* New York: Rinehart and Company, 1960.

Faust, Patricia, L. *Historical Times Illustrated Encyclopedia of the Civil War.* New York: Harper and Row, 1986.

Fehrenbacher, Don E. *Prelude to Greatness: Lincoln in the 1850s.* Calif.: Stanford University Press, 1962.

Fehrenbacher, Don E., and Virginia Fehrenbacher. *Recollected Words of Abraham Lincoln.* Calif.: Stanford University Press, 1996.

Frank, John P. *Lincoln as a Lawyer.* Chicago: Americana House, 1991.

Guelzo, Allen C. *Abraham Lincoln: Redeemer President.* Grand Rapids: William B. Eerdmans, 1999.

———. "Ten True Lies About Abraham Lincoln," part 2, in *For the People: A Newsletter of the Abraham Lincoln Association.* Autumn 2000, vol. 2, no. 3.

Harper, Robert S. *Lincoln and the Press.* New York: McGraw-Hill, 1951.

Hendrick, Burton J. *Lincoln's War Cabinet.* Boston: Little, Brown, 1946.

Herndon, William H., and Jesse W. Weik. *Herndon's Life of Lincoln.* New York: World Publishing Company, 1943 reprint of original.

Holzer, Harold. *The Lincoln-Douglas Debates.* New York: Harper Collins, 1993.

Houser, M. L. *Lincoln's Education and Other Essays.* New Haven, Conn.: Bookman Associates, 1957.

Keckley, Elizabeth. *Behind the Scenes: Thirty Years a Slave and Four Years in the White House.* New York: Oxford University Press, reprint, 1998.

Leidner, Gordon D. *Lincoln on God and Country.* Shippensburg, Pa.: White Mane, 2000.

McPherson, James. *Battle Cry of Freedom.* Oxford University Press, 1988.

Miers, Earl Schenk, ed. *Lincoln Day by Day: A Chronology, 1809–1865.* Washington, D.C.: Lincoln Sesquicentennial Commission, 1960.

Neely, Mark E. *The Abraham Lincoln Encyclopedia.* New York: Da Capo, 1982.

Nicolay, John G., and John Hay, eds. *Complete Works of Lincoln*. New York: Francis D. Tandy, 1905.

Oates, Stephen. *With Malice Toward None*. New York: Harper and Row, 1977.

Pratt, Harry E. *The Personal Finances of Abraham Lincoln*. Springfield, Ill.: Abraham Lincoln Association, 1943.

Randall, J. G. *Lincoln the President: Springfield to Gettysburg*. New York: Dodd, Mead, and Company, 1946.

———. *Lincoln the President: Midstream*. New York: Dodd, Mead, and Company, 1952.

Randall, Ruth Painter. *Lincoln's Sons*. Boston: Little, Brown, and Company, 1955.

Riddle, Donald Wayne. *Lincoln Runs for Congress*. Springfield, Ill.: Abraham Lincoln Association, 1948.

Simon, Paul. *Lincoln's Preparation for Greatness: The Illinois Legislative Years*. Norman, Okla.: University of Oklahoma Press, 1965.

Steers, Edward. *The Escape and Capture of John Wilkes Booth*. Gettysburg, Pa.: Thomas Publications, 1983.

———. *His Name is Still Mudd: the Case Against Doctor Samuel Alexander Mudd*. Gettysburg, Pa.: Thomas Publications, 1997.

Swanberg, W. A. *First Blood: The Story of Fort Sumter*. New York: Charles Scribner's Sons, 1957.

Tarbell, Ida. *Life of Lincoln, 2 vols*. New York: Lincoln Memorial Association, 1900.

Thomas, Benjamin P. *Abraham Lincoln*. New York: Alfred Knopf, 1952.

———. *Lincoln's New Salem*. Springfield, Ill.: Abraham Lincoln Association, 1934.

Trueblood, Elton. *Abraham Lincoln, Theologian of American Anguish*. New York: Harper and Row, 1973.

Van Doren Stern, Philip. *The Life and Writings of Abraham Lincoln*. New York: The Modern Library, 1940.

Warren, Louis. *Lincoln's Youth: Indiana Years 1816–1830*. New York: Appleton-Century-Crofts, 1959.

Williams, Thomas H. *Lincoln and the Generals*. New York: Alfred A. Knopf, 1952.

Wilson, Douglas, and Rodney Davis, eds. *Herndon's Informants: Letters, Interviews, and Statements About Abraham Lincoln*. Urbana, Ill.: University of Illinois Press, 1998.

Wilson, Douglas L. *Honor's Voice: The Transformation of Abraham Lincoln*. New York: Alfred A. Knopf, 1998.

Wolf, William J. *The Religion of Abraham Lincoln*. New York: Seabury Press, 1963.

— THE AUTHOR —

GORDON LEIDNER has had numerous articles published on the Civil War page of the *Washington Times* and in the *Lincolnian*, the Lincoln Group of the District of Columbia's nationally distributed newsletter. Leidner is a board member of the Abraham Lincoln Institute of the Mid-Atlantic and an officer of the Lincoln Group of the District of Columbia. Leidner is also the author of two previous books, including *Lincoln on God and Country*.

— ALSO BY THE AUTHOR —

LINCOLN ON GOD AND COUNTRY

Gordon Leidner

Introduction by Michael Burlingame

ISBN 978-1-57249-207-3 • Hardcover $19.95

Lincoln on God and Country uses the 16th president's own words to demonstrate why he deserves to be called a man of faith, a friend of the slave, and a guardian of democratic government. The casual reader of history will find the book useful because it merges a short biography of Lincoln with his greatest writing and brief editorial comment. The serious student of history will find it a useful reference of some of Lincoln's greatest quotes on democracy, freedom, and faith.

— COVER ILLUSTRATION —

Harry West © 2001

WHITE MANE PUBLISHING CO., INC.

To Request a Catalog Please Write to:

WHITE MANE PUBLISHING COMPANY, INC.

P.O. Box 708 • Shippensburg, PA 17257

e-mail: marketing@whitemane.com

Printed in the United States
213724BV00001B/2/A